Handwriting

the way to teach it

Rosemary Sassoon

Leopard Learning

Acknowledgements

I would like to thank the many teachers who have contributed ideas that have been quoted in this book, or provided interesting handwriting examples, in particular Mrs Gowers of Ryedene County Primary School in Essex and Mrs Lewis of Halstead County Primary School in Kent for all their help, and the Language and Literacy team and their teachers in Kirklees for the drawings on pages 68–9.

Cover design by Gunnlaugur SE Briem.
Line drawings by Pat Savage

Text © Rosemary Sassoon 1990

Original line illustrations © Pat Savage 1990

First published in 1990 by: Stanley Thornes (Publishers) Ltd
Reprinted by Leopard Learning 1995, 1998

British Library Cataloguing in Publication Data
Sassoon, Rosemary
    Handwriting: the way to teach it.
    1. Children.   Curriculum subjects: Handwriting. Teaching
    I. Title
    372.634

    ISBN 1–899929–00–2

Typeset by Tech-Set, Gateshead, Tyne & Wear
Printed and bound in Great Britain

Contents

Part 3 A system for teaching letters

PART 1

Planning handwriting across the whole school

This book provides a practical and innovative approach to the teaching of handwriting. Its key is the belief that the attitudes and methods of teachers are the vital ingredients in children's handwriting success – far more important than the choice of any particular handwriting model. It is particularly crucial that all the teachers in a school are in agreement about the teaching approach.

With this in mind, the first part of the book provides a flexible planning 'kit' to help you and your school develop and implement your own coherent policy. These suggestions can be used alongside any particular handwriting system already in use, but will provide a coherent action plan for those who have not yet started to formulate a systematic policy for themselves.

1 The priority for handwriting in the curriculum

What is learned about handwriting in the early days at school will affect children for many years to come. Providing enough priority is given to skill training, and handwriting is taught systematically but imaginatively from the start of formal teaching, most children should learn quite easily. As there has been so little guidance on how to teach handwriting for so long, it has now become accepted that it is a problem to teach and to learn. This book suggests that informed and confident teachers should be able to teach the basic movement of letters quite quickly and in such a way that many of the problems that hold children back later on should never occur. This is not a matter of more resources or teaching time, but using them at the right time and in the right way.

Each school will have to decide how to arrange the curriculum to ensure that enough time is allotted for skill training, particularly in the first year of schooling. The more thoroughly handwriting is taught at the beginning the less time will be necessary later on.

2 The relationship between the skill of handwriting and other subjects

In recent years it has been fashionable to allow children to try to copy letters and to record their thoughts from almost their first day at school. The attitude has been to let them play with letters and not correct or teach anything that might inhibit them from expressing their creativity. This may sound delightful, indeed young children's pre-school scribbles are fun for all concerned, but the problems that result from letting this playful attitude to letters continue for too long are only too obvious in our classrooms. Once children can write as much as the letters of their own names, they need to be taught the correct movement of each letter. If this is not done, incorrect movements become habits that are progressively more difficult to alter.

Each school has to decide how to introduce the vital movement training quickly enough so that the most able children do not become frustrated. For those who have not yet started to write, it is easier to give a good foundation within a relatively short time. This can be done through the letter-family technique. This allows a vocabulary of short words to be built up as each group of letters is learned. The temptation to let children try to write down their 'news' each day should be resisted until all the letters can be written with a correct movement in their basic form. Problems can arise with early developers (and their parents). These children are most at risk as they often learn to write at home and may need immediate remedial help to correct movement faults. Their parents will need an explanation, otherwise they may feel that their children are being held back. The children also will need careful handling. They may be proud of their skill, thinking that they have already mastered handwriting.

The fine balance between the standard expected in the 'skill' handwriting class, and in creative writing also needs discussion. It is unrealistic to expect the same level of handwriting when the children's entire concentration is on the letterforms (whether at five or ten years old), and when content and perhaps spelling are uppermost in their minds.

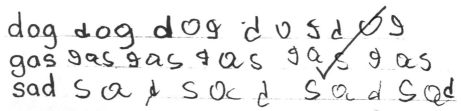

Movement of letters could be corrected in the same way (and at the same time) as spelling.

Most schools already have a realistic outlook on the difference in general quality that might be involved, but what about movement faults? Should they be treated like spelling mistakes and have a correction suggested at the end of a piece of writing? If so, how often can this be done without the risk of inhibiting written expression? Some kind of reminder is however essential to reinforce the correct movement.

3 When to introduce handwriting in the reception class

Not all children may be ready to write when they start school. On the other hand there are dangers in leaving children to experiment for too long on their own. These were explained in the last section. Each school must take its own decision about the right time to begin formal teaching. In some districts the majority of pupils may have had pre-school experience. If they are lucky most children may already have gone through the pre-writing stages and have the capacity to start right away on letters. They may already be used to sitting quietly for a short time to concentrate on a specific task; until this happens little can be achieved. Other schools may have a majority of children with little graphic experience, so that few of the necessary skills required for what is a undoubtedly a difficult task will have been developed. Even for these children a new and more positive attitude to handwriting might be of benefit. In recent years it has been thought in some way wrong to get young children to sit down and learn a skill. The satisfaction of completing a small but suitable task seems to have been forgotten. Handwriting can give this kind of satisfaction, if the suggested systematic method is carried out in an imaginative way and divided into suitably short and reassuringly repetitive lessons.

Pre-writing patterns can help if they are carefully taught, but perhaps the very best way to foster the skills needed for handwriting is actually to begin to teach the simplest letters as early as possible in a formal teaching situation. Little tension is involved when the need for spelling is removed by using patterns of letters rather than words. The necessary distinction between drawing and writing can begin to be established at the same time.

The opposing attitude is that if children are taught to write too young, at too early a stage of their development, they will soon become discouraged by the inadequacy of their own letters. This warning is important and should not be ignored. Those most at risk of discouragement are children who are particularly clumsy. These children will certainly need more encouragement than their peers. It must be understood by everyone in the school that writing may always be a problem for some children, however much help they receive. With that understanding, praise can be given instead of criticism for the extra effort involved. It may be better to foster the necessary graphic skills slowly through graduated experience with letters, than to delay all writing in the hope that skills will develop on their own. Word processors can be magical for young children, but it would be sad if computers were used as an excuse to delay teaching handwriting. Their function should be to take some of the pressure off young children while they develop their skills, or while they tackle specific handwriting and spelling problems.

4 The choice of a handwriting model

The choice of a particular handwriting model must be a whole school decision. First of all there needs to be discussion about whether to have a strict model at all, or to adopt a more liberal attitude to letters. Everyone involved needs to be happy about what they will all have to teach. It must be remembered that at first it may be difficult for some people to change from any other accustomed model.

Four slightly different handwriting models are provided in this book (see pages 6–9). They involve different slants and proportions, as well as alternative forms of some letters. It will not matter if some people dislike some or even all of the letters proposed, because their purpose is to provoke informed discussion about what is essential to teach and what is not. None of them are intended to be models that should be slavishly copied. They illustrate different concepts of letters, and are open to the discussion and criticism that any model should be afforded. Letterforms, even very simple basic ones, are a very personal matter; what one person likes the next may hate. Letters are products of our minds and bodies and reflect our tastes and personalities. Any controversy is welcome in that it supports the underlying purpose of these 'multiple models', which is to suggest that children also perceive and produce the proportions and slant of letters in personal and individual ways from very early on. Perhaps these preferences should be tolerated or even encouraged so that all the teaching emphasis can be placed on the vital training of the correct movements of basic letters, rather than close adherence to any particular model.

These model alphabets provide several alternatives for those letters where there are often stylistic preferences. Some letters, notably 'k', 'f' and 'b' and perhaps 'r', 'v' and 'w' lend themselves to several acceptable variations. A school may want to decide which form of certain letters should be taught, but whichever is chosen it is likely that the children themselves may soon experiment or adapt on their own.

k k k k f f r r q q b b v w v w

Alternatives are provided for several letters and more can be made, such as a short 'f' or angular 'q'.

There is a case for exposing children to the alternatives fairly early on and letting them make the choice, providing all the alternatives are based on acceptable principles. It should be noted, for instance, that the alternatives for the letter 'f' both have descending strokes. Some basic decisions about letterforms need to be taken in order to ensure that the letters that children are first taught and then encouraged to automate, will serve them well all through their school life. If children get used to the idea that 'f' is a short letter they may find it difficult to alter later on. When letters are joined, a short 'f' can easily be confused with a letter 's'.

abcdefghijklmnopqrstuvwxyz

Alphabet 1: Round and upright.

abcdefghijklmnopqrstuvwxyz

Alphabet 2: Round and slanting.

abcdefghijklmnopqrstuvwxyz

Alphabet 3: Oval and upright.

abcdefghijklmnopqrstuvwxyz

Alphabet 4: Oval and slanting.

The differences between the models are particularly noticeable in the letters 'n' and 'o'.

You will notice that the models within this book all have exit strokes on all the letters that terminate on the baseline. Exit strokes help to promote the flowing movement that develops easily into joins. This is in contrast with the stiff straight letters of print script that terminate abruptly on the baseline. When you use a model, you train the hand in a certain movement. Children who are trained to be neat within the precise movement of print script often find it difficult to progress to a flowing joined writing. With straight print script letters maximum pressure is on the baseline, but with an exit the pencil pressure is relaxed as the upstroke changes direction and lifts towards the next letter. This is what promotes a relaxed flowing writing, whether joined or not. An exit stroke also builds in a space between letters.

The decisions that you make for five-year-olds are likely to have a lasting effect, so the choice of some features of a model is a serious matter. At first glance the four alphabets may appear similar. You need to look closely to notice the differences in slant and proportion. It is not usual to have to discriminate between such details, so this choice of model plays its part in helping you to think carefully about letters.

An upright alphabet arranged in letterfamilies

i l t u y j

r n m h b p k

c a d g q o e

s f v w x z

Alternative letters

v w b f f r

q k k k

Characters from the Sassoon family of fonts.

A slanting alphabet arranged in letterfamilies

i l t u y j

r n m h b p k

c a d g q o e

s f v w x z

Alternative letters

v w b f f r

q k k k

Characters from the Sassoon family of fonts.

Capital letters can also be taught in stroke related families

ILT FEH

straight lines

UJ

line and arch

COQGD PRB

circular

NMVWYAKX

diagonal

SZ

counterchange

Characters from the Sassoon family of fonts.

Joins can be taught in similar groups

acdehiklmntu

These letters join easily from the baseline

orvw ft

These letters join from the top or the crossbar

yjgf yjgf

These letters can be joined with loops or not– as you like

bpqu bpqu

These letters can join or not– as you like

zx si is

The letters z and x are best not joined. The letter s can be simplified.

ia ic id ig io iq ie

A join to this group of letters goes over the top and back, except for e

Characters from the Sassoon family of fonts.

One way of using the multiple models

The alphabets, the alternative letters and the family groups on pages 6–9 are arranged in such a way that they can be photocopied. If it is considered desirable to have a model in the reception class, but not to enforce too rigid an attitude to letters, the following three-stage policy can be adopted:

Stage 1

The staff select which of the four suggested models (with any adaptations), and which of the alternative letters are to be used for the children when they are first introduced to writing.

Stage 2

By the time the children have mastered all the letters in family groups and are starting to write spontaneously, they may also be beginning to indicate their preferred slant and letter proportion. When this happens children whose writing is beginning to differ from the chosen model can be offered desk strips from whichever of the three other models most closely resembles their personal writing.

Stage 3

The final step is to let the children produce their own models in the form of desk strips. This gives teachers an opportunity to check that all is well with the children's letters, while giving the pupils the satisfaction of working to their own optimum personal standard. Pupils can update their personal model as often as they like as their handwriting matures.

If you do not like any of the models

Your school may not want to use any of the suggested models. You might feel, despite all the arguments against it, that you do not yet want to change from print script. There could also be special situations where exit strokes are not suitable, such as when children have to learn a second writing system at the same time as a second language. You can still use the alternative letters to help you to choose your own school model; you can trace over the letter groups omitting the exit strokes to make your own master copy. Details of how to use the family groups for introducing handwriting appear on pages 54–9 in Part 3.

The decision to replace print script by letters with an exit stroke is an important one; it may influence children's handwriting for many years to come. It deserves a considerable amount of thought and perhaps a trial period to convince those who are uncertain about its merits.

A more liberal attitude to slant and proportion however is a different kind of decision. Given a free hand children soon indicate their natural slant and letter proportion. Teachers might profit from an opportunity to observe what happens when essentials are taught systematically but the less essential personal features of slant and proportion are allowed to develop naturally. This may well be the best way forward and it is with this in mind that these multiple models have been introduced.

ABCDEFGHIJKLM

Capital letters

NOPQRSTUVWXYZ

The way capital letters are formed is less important as they do not join. Moreover there are individual ways of writing many of them that are quite acceptable.

When the movement is too bizarre, guidance is obviously needed.

The relationship between the movement of capital letters and small letters can be confusing, particularly in the case of 'M' and 'm', and 'N' and 'n', which resemble each other.

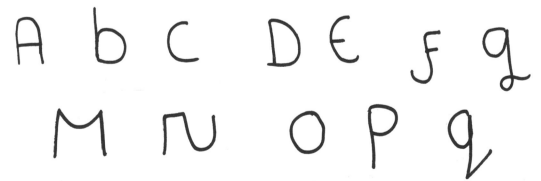

Older children's capitals should be checked from time to time. Look at 'B', 'F', 'G', 'N', 'Q'.

5 Balancing movement and neatness

For too long now neatness has been considered the overriding priority in handwriting. This book seeks to alter this by emphasising, above all, the importance of the correct movement of basic letters. When movement is made top priority and the onward movement from letter to letter is encouraged by teaching integral baseline exit strokes, the result may not be a neat as print script letters. With these priorities however, the most important lessons are being learned first so that there will be no need for re-learning later on. Children will need only to refine and speed up their writing with joins as they progress throughout the six years of primary school. Letters that move correctly can be 'neatened' at any stage by slowing down and concentrating only on appearance, but neat letters with an incorrect movement will prevent joining and cause faster writing to become illegible. It is a matter of sensible balance. There is a time and a place for neatness but too much emphasis on it in the early stages can be counterproductive.

↑M   I am on the pond

Neat printing letters often disguise incorrect movements.

Dear Rachel I hope you have

Letters with forward movement may be less neat than print script.

If you decide on movement as a first priority, then a change of attitude may be needed by all the staff. You will have to praise writing that moves correctly rather than (or as well as) writing that is just beautifully neat. If too much emphasis is put on neatness you will be inhibiting the forward movement that will lead to early joining. It is usually accepted that when children start to join letters their writing looks less neat until they become practised in their joins. With the method that is suggested here the real work is done at the early stages and the results in terms of neatness will be evident later on; the added benefit will be that by the end of primary school the children should have a relaxed and flowing handwriting to serve them well in secondary school and beyond.

Writing this neat is a waste of time.

Writing like this is much better.

This writer has a realistic attitude. Handwriting should be fast as well as legible.

6 How much emphasis on joining

This difficult issue will have to be part of the whole school's policy. For many years in Great Britain little emphasis has been put on joins. Children are supposed to be taught how to join from the time they enter junior school, at about the age of seven years. However with the emphasis elsewhere, either on neatness of the actual letters or only on the content of written work, a large proportion of pupils do not develop a confident joined or semi-joined hand by the time they leave for secondary school. When they are faced with speeding up their writing it all falls apart and many pupils revert to separate letters.

It could be argued that the sensible thing to do is to teach children to join all their letters all the time as was done in this country fifty years ago. This does not seem to work well either. In many countries national models are still based on old-fashioned copperplate writing and children are taught to join all their letters. This seems to work quite well until the need for speed arises. Ten year old pupils may be able to reach a calligraphic standard when writing slowly in a looped cursive, but in secondary school many of them have to revert to printing. Only with luck do they eventually develop a simpler semi-cursive.

tennis, football and cricket. My hair is brown, my skin is brown, and my eyes are hazel. I am tall. My hair is flicked.

The same girl at eleven and thirteen. Her continuous cursive broke down at speed.

The eye is like a camera. lens – cornea colects light. The lens focuses by the muscles.

The reason for this is clear; the hand needs a chance to move along the line, so penlifts are not only permissable but essential during long words. If children are trained to write continuous cursive, they find it not only difficult to alter the movement but difficult to space letters when they do stop for a penlift. You will have to decide how to ensure that all children know how to perform the different joins, without going too far and giving them the idea that they must join every letter all the time. There is at present some talk about the desirability of using continuous cursive to help with the teaching of spelling. This idea needs careful consideration. At the time that such assistance is needed with spelling, the words that the children will be using will probably be limited to four or five letters. When the continuous joining concept and movement is taught from an early age it will last well beyond the stage where it is a help with spelling. Poor spellers often find ten or twelve letter words easier to work out when they are broken up into smaller sections. Something that was taught as a temporary help for young children learning to spell can become a considerable hindrance to the development of an efficient relaxed handwriting, and a disadvantage for more advanced spelling too. Common letter sequences, and common two or three letter words are useful practice when young children are learning to join, but a sensible balance is needed. Children profit by learning to join when it is comfortable and quicker for them to do so, but they also need to understand that penlifts are not only desirable but help make the hand and the writing work more efficiently.

These words were traced by a five-year-old in a school where letters are supposed to be joined from the start. Tracing may be beneficial in certain circumstances but needs careful supervision. This is an example of how ridiculous, and even harmful tracing can be when it encourages the incorrect movement of letters and joins.

Not surprisingly, a year later, pupils in the same school display many letters with an incorrect movement. Children should never be encouraged to join before they have internalised the correct movement of basic letters.

There are two further points to consider: not all young children have the co-ordination to perform more than the simple baseline joins when they start school at the age of five, so a rigid policy of continuous cursive from the start may handicap a proportion of children. Finally, it cannot be repeated too often that children should never be taught joins until all their letters move correctly.

7 Display writing – both by teachers and pupils

[handwritten annotation: print vs cursive]

One final argument in favour of print script remains to be dispelled. It is that handwriting should look like the print in early reading books. Children see letters of all kinds on television and in advertisements and soon learn to decipher the different forms of the various letters. Having thus disposed of the need to teach print-like letters for the sake of recognition, this is a good moment to look at all the letterforms that appear on the school walls. If you are going to use a model that has exit strokes on all letters that terminate on the baseline, then you will need to make sure that all handwritten exemplars have exit strokes.

You are going to need a coherent policy for all display writing. It may be difficult for teachers who have long been used to writing print script to be consistent in producing separate letters with exit strokes. In fact this is exactly what children have had to do for so long – to change from print script to letters with 'hooks' on them before they are able to join. Teachers should be able to feel as well as see the difference in the letters so that they understand the reason for the change in policy. It may not be so easy to write separate letters (or joined ones) that are free of personal eccentricities. Children are quick to copy and often exaggerate any such quirks, but in coming to terms with their own handwriting, teachers will gain invaluable insight into the kinds of problems that their pupils have to face.

If you are encouraging children to join up their letters, you will have to decide if and when joined writing should be used on the blackboard or on classroom notices. The argument against using joined writing in the classroom has always been that it is more difficult for children to read. This may be valid in certain cases such as children with learning difficulties, but even so it is often claimed that joined letters emphasise the word shape and help recognition. Anyhow it is rather a negative attitude when pupils are being encouraged to join their own letters. Providing the adult writing is kept clear and simple it should help those children who are beginning to join their letters and will certainly provide them with a good example.

The priority that you are giving to the correct movement of letters rather than to conventional neatness may lead to new attitudes to the examples of pupils' handwriting on display. You will be praising and therefore displaying examples where the writing moves freely and begins to join quite early on. If you require particularly neat examples for a special occasion you can explain that all through life we need 'special occasion' handwriting as well as everyday handwriting. Important letters have to be drafted and redrafted as grammar and spelling are improved, and it is usually only the final one that is copied out slowly to ensure the best possible layout and handwriting. In this way you can encourage a high standard without leaving children with the idea that all writing must be perfect, because that requires too much concentration on neatness when more emphasis should be on content.

Children need to be taught how to lay out a page. Special occasions provide ideal opportunities to show how much difference good presentation can make.

8 Liaison with pre-school groups, parents and other schools

When you have formulated your new policy it is a good idea to let both associated pre-school groups and parents know what you have decided and why. It will help if all concerned know that capital letters are not the best way to teach pre-school children to write. It is also helpful if pre-school groups can make sure that if children are writing their own names they are shown the correct movement of those letters. It may be unrealistic to expect parents to monitor the movement of their young children's first letters, but both parents and pre-school groups can play an important part in teaching pre-writing skills. A demonstration in the form of a 'new parents' evening may be effective; it provides an opportunity to explain the importance of the correct movement. If all concerned understand the concepts behind the alphabet these vital ideas can be demonstrated and practised informally. In this way children are prepared for the task that awaits them on entering school. These ideas, such as left-to-right movement and discrimination between heights and mirror images, can be introduced in informal situations. They can be explored kinaesthetically through three dimensional play with whatever materials are available in the home or playgroup, as well as visually.

When it comes to the first year at school, parents need to understand that the emphasis on the movement of writing means that the handwriting may not appear as neat as their older children's print script did. The children will be better off in the end as they have plenty of time to refine their writing without having to alter their letters. If you decide to allow children to start to join their letters as soon as appropriate, then again explanation will be needed. Parents who themselves may never have been taught to join can respond by claiming that this emphasis on handwriting is repressive. They need an explanation that your skill lessons are not reverting to old-fashioned ideas, but making life easier for their children in the long term. As parents begin to understand how important it is for children to have adequate writing and how difficult it is for them when they begin, those same parents will start to realise the part that they might play in helping their pre-school children. In the developed world young children are given fewer and fewer real tasks to perform before they go to school. Their hand-eye co-ordination is not developed nor the important discrimination that is needed to recognise or reproduce details of letters. Television may widen childrens' general knowledge but it does not give them the foundation for accurate skills. Parents who realise this can do so much to help their children by playing all the tried and tested old-fashioned games that develop these faculties, and by giving time to help pre-school children with real tasks around the home or garden.

How this information is spread is obviously up to individual schools, but many infant schools already provide lively leaflets to explain what they are trying to do and how parents can help.

Pre-school groups and parents can help with specific pre-writing exercises if they are informed of the importance of such concepts as directionality and mirror images. They can then ensure that children learn the correct movement of the letters at least within their own names. This child has both directionality and letter movement problems.

Names may need more attention later on. They are often the first letters that children attempt to join.

   Liaison between primary schools in the same area can also be a great help. Not only can they produce a uniform policy that will benefit their pupils but they can also pool resources such as inservice training sessions and learn from each others experiences. If primary and secondary schools were to meet occasionally there could be even greater benefits. Feedback can be available to junior schools to show any difficulties that their own (ex)pupils are having in dealing with the speed, pressure and new priorities in secondary schools. A positive consequence may be modifications in the policy for top juniors, with more emphasis on speed to prepare them for the changeover. Together the schools can discuss the real problem: that unless pupils have learned the correct movement of basic letters it is inadvisable for them to be encouraged to join up their writing. At whatever stage basic movement faults are detected they must be dealt with, but teachers must also be aware that determining the rights and wrongs of personal movement between letters is not so straightforward. Many personal joins remain perfectly legible and enable pupils to speed up their writing. All of this points to the need for teachers of all subjects to be more informed about handwriting.

9 A policy for left-handers

Left-handers need consideration, especially in the early years when they are forming their handwriting strategies. In countries where left-hander's needs are written into the curriculum it appears that far fewer of them end up with problems. Handwriting problems have such far-reaching effects on all school work that unless care is taken with our left-handed pupils, some may not achieve their potential. The commonsense rules are well documented. In essence they are as follows:

1. Paper should be placed to the writers left side, then slanted to suit each individual. This allows writers to have their hand below the line, in a non-inverted position, without interrupting their line of vision.

2. Free-flowing modern pens that do not smudge are recommended for left-handers.

3. A seat high enough to allow the writers to see over their hand is a help, and appropriate lighting to make sure that left-handers are not writing in the shadow of their own hand.

4. The pen needs to be held far enough from the point to allow the writer to see the written trace. This may result in a feeling of loss of control, but it is only the thumb that gets in the way; the index finger can be as near to the point as the writer wishes.

Many of these points are dependent on the teacher; for instance the children cannot place the paper to their left side if there is not enough space at the table, or if they are sitting on their right-handed neighbour's right side. Left-handers will all be writing in the shadow of their own hand if the room is organised for right-handers.

There are other more subtle points that are seldom mentioned. Many books are arranged with the material to copy on the left side and the space on the right side. This will mean that left-handers may be covering the copy as they write. Copybooks could be designed for left-handers with the layout reversed: the blank page for writing on the left side and the information to be copied on the right side.

Most left-handers need to place their paper to their left side so they can see what they have written. Otherwise they may bend over sideways or twist their wrist above the line of writing.

What about a special model for left-handers? Many young children will produce writing that slopes backwards as it is more difficult for left-handers to slant their letters forwards. Why should they always be confronted with a model that they may not be able to follow? One with a slight backwards slant may encourage them.

It is difficult for left-handers to follow the movements when they are demonstrated by a right-hander. Teachers should try to demonstrate individually to left-handers using their left hand. The resulting writing may not be very neat but it will help pupils. It could also help right-handers to understand the specific problems that left-handers face.

backward sloping

A backward-sloping model might encourage left-handers whose writing slants backwards.

Though criticised at school, this left-hander could not alter her slant. Changing her paper position might help but the necessary manipulation of the fingers is lacking.

Some left-handers may experience directional problems and will need special attention. Their difficulties are not easily understood. If, for example, right-handers try to write with their left hand they may find, as most left-handers do, that it is easiest to draw a line from right to left. All children need to be taught that writing (and reading) go from left to right, but left-handers may need much more practice in left-to-right exercises before this becomes the automatic response to an empty page. Some kind of visual reminder may be a good idea. This can be a simple red margin or red strip put at the left side of each page, or something more fun as suggested on page 71. Letter movement may be a problem too. Left-handers seem to find the clockwise movement easier than the anti-clockwise one that is needed for so many letters. The letter 'o' is often a problem and this may affect the associated letters 'a' 'd' 'g' and 'q' as well. In some cases the right-to-left movement of some or even all letters may go undetected for several years. Pupils get used to starting letters at the place where they would normally end. This is bad enough with separate letters, but the real difficulties appear when pupils find that they cannot join their letters. It may not be easy to detect this movement problem. Extra-wide or uneven spacing between letters can also be an indicator, but older pupils manage to adapt so it may not be obvious unless the writer is watched in action. Once such problems are diagnosed it may be a long time before writers are able to alter the movement of their letters. Early detection and remediation are vital. All these aspects need to be woven into a policy that spreads awareness of left-handers' needs and ensures that they are met.

10 A policy for special needs

Most schools designate one teacher to be responsible for special needs. This does not always mean that the chosen teacher has received the thorough training that is needed to diagnose and then deal with the complex problems that are so prevalent in our schools. Ideally children should have their problems diagnosed accurately and receive adequate individual attention and remedial help from informed specialists. Even this would probably not be enough; all the good done in individual sessions can be destroyed quite easily when the children return to the classroom.

Children with learning difficulties have very little self-confidence, and this lack of confidence will be mirrored in their handwriting. They will have little control over the tensions that can distort their letters, so any policy has to involve co-operation between teachers. This should ensure that children with real problems meet with encouragement and sympathy and not too much criticism in their every-day work.

A shark is the single serious predator of the planet. In the stomach great white this seals and sealion was found.

Clumsy children cannot help their awkwardness being reflected in their handwriting.

Within a school it should not be difficult to keep class and subject teachers aware of any areas where reinforcement and encouragement might be beneficial, but difficulties can arise when children are released from class for individual tuition, or have such tuition outside school hours.

Many children, whose learning difficulties show through in their handwriting, have organisational difficulties too. The word 'dyspraxia' is often used to describe this condition which may affect the organisation of physical actions and hence handwriting. Such organisational problems can overlap into other areas of daily life. Children who are affected, may for example, continually forget their homework or leave their sports equipment at home. They may have difficulty copying notices from the board, and should they have missed instructions because they were out of the classroom for extra tuition, any resulting confusion can be magnified. Putting on clothes may present a complicated ordeal, and remembering messages a near impossibility. A school might find it useful to keep in close contact with parents to minimise such problems. In extreme cases a computerised pocket organiser can help.

A policy for special needs means that everyone has a part to play in supporting children with problems without disrupting the smooth running of the school.

11 A policy for newcomers from other schools

New pupils may join the school at any time so there will always be decisions to make about how to assess and integrate newcomers. It is not easy for a child coming to a new school. Everything may be different and one of the most visible differences can be the handwriting. If there is a policy of ensuring the correct movement of letters then some kind of tactful assessment will be needed to see that a new pupil's letters have no important movement faults. That will be relatively easy once teachers become adept at spotting, explaining and dealing with such matters, but stylistic differences or joining differences need more thought. Supposing children had been taught a somewhat idiosyncratic italic while your pupils had had a less strict or obvious model? Supposing that they had either learned a continuous looped cursive, or at the other extreme had become confirmed in a fast print script, at the age when your children were being shown how to join as and where comfortable? Should the new pupils be encouraged to follow what the other children were doing, or continue their original taught model? Some newcomers may wish to conform as soon as possible, in which case they deserve the extra help to make any alterations. This might be the case where a top junior child had not yet started to join any letters. Other pupils may be both happy and competent in their habitual model, in which case it will be unfair and to their disadvantage to expect them to alter. In practice this more liberal attitude means more work for teachers. They need to be informed of the details of the different writing models and how some of them may need to be modified so that older pupils can develop a fast personal handwriting.

It is not only children who may be affected by changing schools. Teachers who may have come from a school with quite different views on handwriting may also need guidance. If they have not been trained how to detect and deal with movement problems they should be made aware of the importance of this part of the school policy, whatever the age of the pupils that they are to teach. Stylistic differences may not be such a problem. It might be quite useful for older pupils to be exposed to another style of writing, provided it moves correctly and is free of personal idiosyncracies. It is notoriously difficult for an adult to become consistent in a new handwriting model. This difficulty could be explained to the pupils as another lesson on the realities of writing. It might be far better for an unusual form of a letter – for instance 'f' – to become a point of discussion than for the teacher to be trying unsuccessfully to mimic a model that is unfamiliar.

With young children, however, it may be necessary to be more consistent with such details as exit strokes on letters. Where this is an important part of the school policy new teachers should be encouraged to practise this until exit strokes become more or less automatic. This means not only on the blackboard but when marking children's books as well.

lay in Virginia

If italic is perceived or produced as a zig-zag, resulting problems can be difficult to retrain.

an am an am

It is difficult to adapt to a model that does not come naturally.

I hate the knew kind of writing

This seven-year-old had round writing and hated the new oval model.

I hate the knew kind

We had a pleasant walk today
Over the hills and far away

This seven-year-old had to follow the school model, but her natural writing was narrower.

We had a pleasant walk today, offer if for
Over the hills and far away

If for and offer left
lf for offer left

Adults also have problems. This teacher's personal crossbar, rising diagonally from below the baseline, misled her into teaching the 'f' join in the school model along the baseline.

12 Terminology

Unfortunately there is at present no adequate and universally agreed terminology to describe the various features of handwriting. Even the terminology to describe the stages of children in school varies considerably, not only between countries but within them. (The terms used in this book are set out below.) However, it is important within any one school to have and to use consistent and sufficiently precise terms, so that everyone understands exactly what is being discussed. Different kinds of letters need naming. Should letters still be referred to as 'upper and lower case' after the outdated way that typographers stored their lead type, or should more child-orientated terms such as 'capital and small letters' be used? Parts of letters have specific names, and once these are defined there can be a much clearer idea of the complexities of handwriting. The lines that mark the heights of letters also need defining and in doing so teachers may become aware of the importance of height differentials.

Terms that describe joining are often inadequate and can lead to misunderstanding. Print and cursive are two terms that are frequently used to describe unjoined or joined writing respectively. Print has other connotations and can be taken to refer to the straight forms of 'print script', thus perpetuating the myth that these are the only letters that young children should be exposed to. The term 'cursive' can have several meanings and none of them are precise. To some people the word suggests the old-fashioned looped writing, where every letter is supposed to be joined all the time. Other people take the term to describe the simplified cursive introduced by Marion Richardson, where descenders are never meant to join. Others think it just means joined-up, and only when they are asked how much joining does this suggest, or how often are there pen-lifts in their own writing do they begin to comprehend how imprecise this term is. Separate letters, letters that touch, and letters that join may all be present and quite acceptable in a short passage of writing. More precise terms such as continuous cursive or semi-cursive may lead to a better understanding of how an efficient personal writing works.

'The movement of writing' is a term used in this book. The use of this phrase may be unfamiliar to those who have always judged letters by their formation or perhaps

Terms relating age to the year and level in schools

Year	Age	Level	Other terms used in this book
1–2	5–6	Infant	Reception, middle infants, top infants
3–6	7–10	Junior	First-year juniors to top juniors
7–13	11–18	Secondary	

Some terms relating to letters

Parts of letters

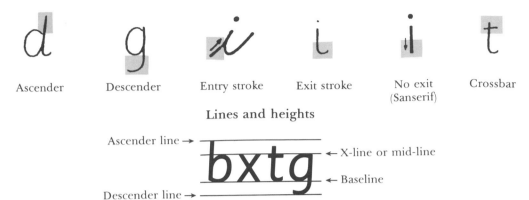

| Ascender | Descender | Entry stroke | Exit stroke | No exit (Sanserif) | Crossbar |

Lines and heights

Ascender line →

← X-line or mid-line

bxtg

← Baseline

Descender line →

Different kinds of letters

Print script
(Written sanserif letters)

hid

Written letters with exit strokes

hid

A sanserif typeface (helvetica bold)

hid

Sassoon Primary typeface
(Sanserif, ascending strokes
and baseline exit strokes)

hid

Semi-cursive
(Marion Richardson)

fly eight

Continuous looped cursive

yes bet

Some aspects of letters have specific terms but what do we call ordinary writing that is usually a mixture of joined, touching and separate letters, developed by individuals to suit themselves and their tasks?

The importance of movement both on and off the paper

Movement on the paper	Movement both off and on paper

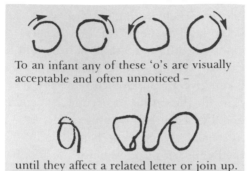

To an infant any of these 'o's are visually acceptable and often unnoticed –

until they affect a related letter or join up.

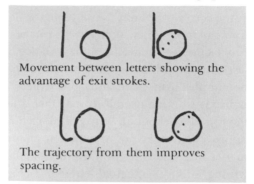

Movement between letters showing the advantage of exit strokes.

The trajectory from them improves spacing.

The movement of the hand when the pen is on the paper produces what we see as letters. The movements that the hand performs when it is off the paper are just as important because this can influence the efficiency as well as the spacing of letters.

their shape. The word 'movement' ties the letters to the hand that writes, so that it is easy to explain that the hand is being trained in a movement. Shape or even formation when used in relation to letters, are more static descriptors that could ignore the vital direction or trajectory of the strokes that make up our written letters. Maybe it is imprecise terminology that has led to the present position where the incorrect movement of letters is so prevalent in our children's handwriting. The importance of movement is not appreciated and movement faults are often ignored.

A discussion of terminology in any staffroom may reveal any other misunderstandings. Developing a working terminology within the school can do more than clarify the meaning of words; it may provide the insight to observe the details of what is actually happening in the classroom.

Children need to have consistent terms used in the classroom. It is suggested on page 45 that in the early years children can invent their own words for some of the aspects of handwriting, and these can be adopted in the classroom. This should be encouraged as it brings the subject to life, but any newcomers to the school, whether staff or pupils, may need those terms defining.

The term 'writing' itself is used in different ways. A complaint at the end of an essay saying 'badly written' may apply either to handwriting or to content, or even to both. Handwriting may be criticised as 'messy' because of frequent erasures. In some cases poor spelling would be the real cause of the untidy page and all the rubbings-out. 'Untidy' can refer as much to the layout of a page as to the letters themselves. All this imprecise criticism is of little help to the unhappy writer who may not know how or what to improve.

The term 'correct' may also be confusing in relation to handwriting. What is correct other than the correct movement of basic letters? Many preconceived ideas of what is conventionally correct or incorrect, whether referring to letters or to such matters as penhold, may be personal and subjective. All these matters need unemotional examination - but informed discussion requires precise terms.

13 Assessment and record keeping

Some record of pupils' handwriting is desirable, especially during the early years of implementing a new policy. This can be at a class level as the job of each teacher. Any examples should be representative of writing for different tasks. There should be fast writing perhaps from dictation, and slow, show writing as well. There should also be samples from good and poor writers. This can give a realistic picture of how a policy is working overall. It may take a few years for the results to become evident at the top of a school, in terms of more flowing and efficient handwriting. Such improvement may never be able to be proven statistically, other perhaps than in the matter of a reduction in movement faults. When children begin to enjoy the act of writing, when their actual letters reflect a more relaxed attitude and when their personal handwriting gains in speed and confidence to enable them to express their thoughts freely (and legibly) on paper, all the effort will have been worthwhile. Norms should not be taken too seriously. Pupils need eventually to acquire a mature writing that suits their own needs and personality, at school and later in life, and they cannot and should not have to conform to a common measure.

Children get satisfaction from keeping samples of their own writing and watching it improve. If schools adopt the idea of children producing their own model strips, then perhaps pupils should be encouraged to keep these, along with other examples, in a special handwriting folder. If children are encouraged to judge their own handwriting, for their own benefit, they may develop the self-criticism and motivation that is needed to make real progress.

Names written shortly after entering school in September and again three months later. A record like this is satisfying for both pupil and teacher. It is a justification for a systematic method of teaching, and proof (two of many such examples from this school) that it is quite possible to alter the movement of young children's letters.

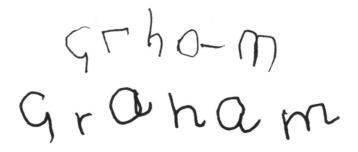

PART 2

Classroom management

Classroom management involves a careful consideration of the materials to be used and everything that affects writing posture. This includes penhold and paper position, as well as appropriate furniture and the choice of pens. These factors are as important as the letters that are written – and inevitably affect them. This section will provide you with a clear analysis of the issues and practical suggestions for improvements.

14 Layout of the classroom

Many, perhaps most, infant schools adopt an informal classroom layout with small groups of children seated around tables. There are, however, those who from choice or necessity have a more formal arrangement. When it comes to teaching handwriting, or for that matter any other subject that involves copying from the board, the way children are ranged around the classroom and their individual angle to the blackboard become important issues. It is well known that many young children have difficulty relating one plane to another, so they may find difficulty in copying from the blackboard. This can be exacerbated if they have to twist around to see the board and then back again to their paper. Some children with visual difficulties may find it difficult to see at all from certain angles. For many classroom activities the family group situation, around a table, is ideal for young children. In handwriting this might not be the case if or when instruction is from the board.

Teacher's suggestion: 'We group the children around tables for most activities, but re-arrange the room for any formal teaching that involves copying from the board.'

Lighting is also important, and left-handers in particular may be disadvantaged in some classroom situations. This can occur in more formal arrangements where desks are aligned. If the classroom is arranged with the light coming from the side best suited to the right-handed majority, then left-handers may all end up writing in the shadow of their own hand. Adequate lighting is always important; what may be enough light at adult height is not always sufficient for young children. If they become accustomed to hunching over their work in order to see what they are doing, this habit can become hard to break and last for many years.

These matters need to be considered when formulating a policy, and to be reviewed from time to time.

15 Balancing whole class instruction with one-to-one attention

Some aspects of handwriting can and even should be taught to the whole class at the same time. Practising the movement of letters in the air with a whole-arm movement can even be done in the gym or playground, and certainly is a whole class activity. The initial introduction to the simplified letter families can also be done from the front of the class. The teacher can demonstrate the letter sequences carefully on the board, talking through the movement and height differentials at the same time. However, as in any other skill training, there must be a certain amount of one-to-one instruction. Experienced teachers take this in their stride. They employ various strategies for dividing the class into groups and ensuring that some are happily engaged in an activity that does not need supervision, or else they make use of classroom aides. These teachers realise the importance of keeping a close check on such important matters as the movement of letters. They know only too well that some children do not manage to translate what is taught from the front of the class onto a sheet of paper. They manage to get round to children individually to watch them form their letters. This is the only way of ensuring correct movement.

It is not possible to tell from a previously written sample whether a letter 'i' or 'l' was started at the top or the bottom. In the early days children profit from seeing a letter written for them by the teacher at their own place and on their own paper. This may be specially relevant to left-handers who can find it difficult to copy from the movement of a right-handed teacher at the blackboard. In such cases it is a great help for teachers to demonstrate individually to left-handers with their left hand, however shaky the resulting letters may be.

As far as handwriting is concerned, there is likely to be more difference between the most able and the least advanced pupil in a reception class than at any other time in school. Some children may write quite well before they arrive, while others have seldom even held a pencil. This is another good reason for small groups working together for short periods under close supervision. Differences in development or experience may call for quite different approaches, at least for a while.

There is another problem when trying to teach the essential basics of a skill from the front of the class: the whole attention of all the children is required. This may be a considerable problem in any schools where young children have not been accustomed to sitting still and paying attention.

An experienced teacher's method: '*Five-year-olds feel the need for constant attention. I found that by being very firm and saying 'please wait, I will see your work in a minute', they got used to the idea that handwriting is very important. They also realised that they were to get my undivided attention shortly, and that I see everyone in turn. It was hard at first but by the end of the first term the children enjoyed the routine and complained on the few days when it was broken.*'

16 Posture

At all ages and stages posture plays an important part in how children write (and also how they may scan for reading). Everyone involved with children needs to be aware of this, and also aware that posture itself can provide useful clues to children's difficulties. A floppy posture may only indicate boredom, but tension is often mirrored in the way a child sits. Children may not be able to sit upright when misery is contorting their body. Unusual visual problems of the kind that are not detected in ordinary school eye tests can occasionally be detected from the way children sit or tilt the head. A rigid right or wrong attitude to posture cannot work as eyes, backs and body proportions all need to be taken into consideration, but the specific points about furniture and paper position that are raised in this section always need to be dealt with.

These issues need to be considered not only by reception teachers but by everyone in the school. Once teachers are made aware of such possibilities they go into their classrooms and begin to notice what is happening to their own children. This awareness is more important than any set of rules because noticing, reacting, adapting and seeing the improvement in their own pupils is the best way of convincing all those who deal with children of the importance of such matters.

Children need furniture of an appropriate height. This small five-year-old has her chin on the table and is having to twist her hand in order to see what she is writing — a particularly inauspicious start for a left-hander. Bad postural habits soon become automatic.

17 Appropriate furniture

Individual teachers may not have much say in the choice of furniture for the classroom. In many schools such matters are dealt with by the local education authority supplies department. A certain degree of flexibility can usually be arranged within schools, so it is essential to be aware of the importance of furniture and the effects of inappropriate chairs or tables on children's posture, comfort and eventually their writing performance. Muscles all up the arm and even in the back work together to produce the written trace of the hand movement that we call handwriting. How children sit has an important part to play in the development of personal handwriting strategies.

Children cannot sit comfortably and use their hands and bodies effectively if chairs or tables are either too high or too low. They may begin to adapt their bodies accordingly and once an awkward body posture becomes habitual it may not improve even when appropriate furniture is eventually provided. Some pupils may be so affected that their discomfort turns to pain. Hands, arms or necks can hurt so much that some children may almost stop writing.

In any classroom there are likely to be children of widely different sizes. The difference between the largest and the smallest may be considerable yet the children are expected to work at the same sized tables or chairs. When it is suggested that different sized chairs and tables could be provided within each classroom teachers respond in different ways. Some report ingenious ways that they have already devised of managing this.

Teacher's idea: *'In our school each size of furniture is of a different colour. We arrange for exchanges between the classes but do not refer to larger or smaller sizes as some children are unhappy about their excessively large or small stature being referred to. We colour code the chairs and suggest who should use which colour.'*

Some teachers complain that a wide variety of furniture in a classroom may appear less tidy than chairs and tables of all one size, but the pupils' needs should come first. This involves varying the size of both chairs *and* tables; it is not just a matter of large chairs for small children or smaller chairs for large children in order to sit comfortably at a table. (This solution would leave the smallest children with their legs dangling in mid air whilst the largest pupils would find that the lower part of their legs were cramped.) Tables of different heights may be needed. A rough guide to a comfortable table height is that writers should be able to rest their arms on the table without raising their shoulders or rounding their backs.

A few teachers who have adopted a liberal attitude to furniture report that problem children occasionally use chair size as an excuse for disruption, refusing to sit until they are seated in their own chair. Undoubtedly a sensible balance has to be achieved, but once observant teachers become aware of the desirability of appropriate furniture, they soon notice those in most need of help.

A sloping board supports the arm and is effective in minimising tremor. The girl above had cerebral palsy. The optimum angle will vary from writer to writer. Most people would benefit from having a slanting surface to write on. Desk-sized sloped boards are easily constructed, but any piece of hardboard resting on the lap, or supported on the table by a book, provides a temporary solution. In the classroom a loose-leaf binder with the fatter side away from the writer can give easy and unobtrusive support.

Slanting surfaces were once in general use in classrooms but have now given way to flat tables. It is unlikely that this decision will be reversed, but undoubtedly, as scribes and calligraphers over the centuries have demonstrated, it is better for the hand to write when it is supported by a slanting board or desk. For anyone with a tremor a considerable slant can be a great help. The more the arm is supported the better control the writer may have over a tremor. It is possible to buy ready-made desks but simple ones as illustrated here can easily be constructed. In severe cases a table that is adjustable both for height and slant can provide the best solution. These are easily obtainable from artist's suppliers or, probably more expensively, from medical catalogues. We need a flexible attitude to writing posture when real problems intervene.

Teacher's question concerning a young spina bifida child in an ordinary classroom, whose doctor recommended that the child should work standing up:

'Surely a child cannot write when standing up?'.

Answer: *'That is exactly what clerks did in the last century. Their high desks, rather like enlarged lecterns, can often be found in antique shops. A similar one was soon constructed for this child.'*

18 Paper position and its effect on posture

The issue of paper position and how it can affect a writer's posture need to be understood. It may be easy enough to explain that most children, in order to sit comfortably to write, and at the same time to see what they are doing, should have their paper over to the side of the hand that they write with. That means that right-handers need their paper over to the right side, and more importantly, left-handers need their paper over to their left side. Children can then slant their paper if they wish. There can be no absolute rule because it is not always the hand that has to be considered. In some cases the paper position might need to be different to take visual problems or unusual body proportion into account.

If the majority need to place their paper to one side, allowing their arms to move freely, then they also need enough space. This is one more thing think about.

If left-handers want to sit next to their right-handed friends then they will need reminding to sit to the left of their right-handed neighbour to avoid bumping into each other.

A child soon becomes used to a particular paper position. In this case the paper was centrally placed at a considerable slant, as recommended in this school's policy. Notice the size of the exercise book.

A junior school child's idea for a reminder when left- and right-handers want to sit together: 'Don't knock funny bones.'

All aspects of handwriting soon become automated. If children are not taught where to place their paper when they first start to learn to write, they may, for whatever reason, get used to placing it somewhere unsuitable. The body then adjusts itself to the accustomed paper position, often contorting itself in the process. It should be the other way round: the paper should be placed to suit the writer.

Children profit from experimenting to find out what suits them best. Experiencing what it feels like to have the paper in the worst possible position can be beneficial. Those who need extra reinforcement could have 'corners' of coloured tape stuck on their desk to remind them of their paper position. Another way to do this would be to use a paper overlay, rather like an enlarged place mat, with the recommended paper position for a particular child marked on it in some 'fun' way.

A teacher's idea: 'Our class is equipped with hexagonal tables that do not allow much space for children to learn the best way to place their paper for writing. When the class is divided into groups we use the only rectangular table in the room for the group that is concentrating on handwriting.'

When the writer's arms grew she twisted the paper (and her body) further and further round. The initial cue to slant the paper seemed to override the more sensible solution of moving the paper to the right.

19 Penhold

Penhold is perhaps the most difficult issue to tackle today. It is important that schools understand the complex issues at stake before they decide on a policy. Most writing manuals are still advocating the virtues of a traditional tripod penhold. There are numerous products from triangular pencils to ingenious plastic grips to fasten over both pens and pencils. These reinforce traditional penholds and retrain what are termed 'unconventional' ones. Most books recommend that when training a child to hold a pencil the index finger should be extended so that it is the digit closest to the pencil point. This finger position should prevent excess pressure on the joints of the index finger. An extended forefinger is also an advantage in directing the pencil because it permits free movement, particularly in the directions that lead to an oval slanting writing. Unfortunately, the issue at the present time is far from being as straightforward as these instructions for penhold suggest. Children usually formulate their mark-making strategies before they reach school age, and today a traditional pencil has often been replaced in the home by felt-tipped or other modern markers.

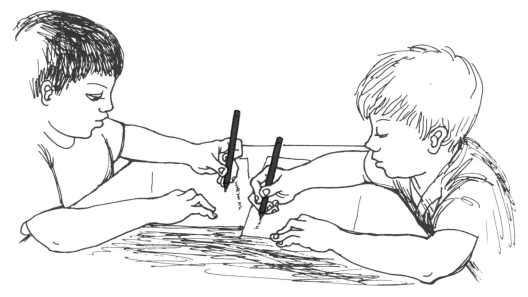

A left- and a right-hander trying out different strategies to get their upright felt-tipped pens to work.

These modern pens work at a different elevation from pencils, so they need a different penhold to allow them to be almost upright. The more worn out a felt pen becomes the more it requires to be held upright in order to produce any trace at all. Even during school hours children may spend as much time using a modern colouring stick (for want of a better word) than a traditional pencil. So, if we want efficient penholds, it may be necessary to teach different strategies for different writing implements. Left to themselves children develop compromise strategies that sometimes work well for the writer but invite criticism from teachers and others.

There is an alternative penhold where the pen is held between the index and middle fingers. This works well for left- as well as right-handers and allows the pen to adjust comfortably to any angle. This boy is just experimenting with it. Had he been introduced to it earlier he might have avoided getting into the habit of half twisting his hand above the line of writing.

When children get older, and are so set in their ways that it is hard to change, certain unconventional penholds show their disadvantages. They may not allow the writing to be speeded up, they may restrict the production of certain strokes so that letterforms become distorted, and they may even cause pain under pressure.

There is an alternative penhold (shown above) that would allow any writing implement, traditional or modern, to be held in such a way that it could function efficiently and with little strain on the hand, at any desired angle. It is far too early to suggest that it should be introduced into all infant classes, as there may be other disadvantages to it, but it is a useful answer to many children's difficulties.

My advice must also be that the whole hand has to be considered; whether it should be on edge or slightly flattened (but not too flat or too much on edge). What happens at the wrist is just as important as what the fingers are doing. If the wrist starts to twist at an early age then the hand may not perform precision movements with as much freedom as it could when not inverted or twisted. All of these features are inextricably involved with other aspects of writing posture. An inverted (twisted wrist) position, especially in a right-hander, is almost always the result of not having the paper over to the side of the writing hand. If schools persist in teaching or allowing a central paper position, then they are producing the situation that they then deplore. What one teacher may see as the pencil pointing towards the child and digging into the paper is usually the result of a twist of the wrist. It is always necessary to look for the cause and not only to try to deal with the symptom.

With this attitude in mind, you can go into classrooms and start observing childrens' hands. If the children manage well with a traditional penhold then encourage this, but if they cannot or do not normally achieve this then you must

The way the pen is held will affect the letters that are produced. This stiff inverted hand position resulted in extraordinary clockwise letters that looped backwards (See above.)

question why. Is it the proportions of their hands, is it previously learned strategies perhaps influenced by felt-tipped pens or possibly a developmental factor that makes pencil control more difficult in some cases? Or is it a sign of a particular child's inner tensions? There are many different issues to consider. Why, for instance, do so many children hold their pencils so close to the point that they cannot see what they are doing? Ask them and you may get the answer that I usually get: 'Because it is easier to control.' Closer inspection may then reveal that the pupil's hand is on edge and indeed it may be more difficult to control a pencil like that. If you analyse the situation carefully you may conclude that it does not matter if the forefinger remains close to the point to help with control; after all, it is only the thumb that obstructs the line of vision. The simple solution may be to move the thumb up the pencil handle so that everyone is happy.

I am suggesting that it is more valuable to approach such problems with an open mind rather than blindly to follow techniques suited to writing implements that no longer predominate. One thing is certain: if you want to help children to alter their penhold to one that might work better for them, it is important to have a very clear idea of why and how to go about it. If you cannot explain the reason for change coherently, and demonstrate the advantages effectively, then you will have little success in altering previously learned strategies.

Schools will themselves have to decide whether to try to hold back the advance of modern implements and insist on pupils using only traditional nibbed pens. Unfortunately we cannot rely on manufacturers to research their products in such depth as to provide us with helpful answers. Once again it is up to teachers to do their best to help children to find strategies that will serve them well, both at school and beyond, in the wider world.

20 Materials: pencils and pens, paper size and lines

The materials that are to be used for handwriting throughout the school need to be planned as carefully as all the other items in the policy. In the past, decisions on such matters as pencil size, shape or point have often been taken without discussion within the school and certainly without consulting the preferences of the pupils. A simple survey usually shows that there are strongly held preferences from an early age, and that many young children dislike the fat pencils that have been supplied to infant schools for many years. Given a free choice, pupils soon demonstrate what best suits their hands and their handwriting. It is not always the same for every child, and there are many different shaped pencils on the market: fat ones, thin ones, hexagonal or triangular ones. Then there is the pencil point to consider: soft, medium or hard. A trial pack of half a dozen different types of pencils should soon show up those that are the most popular with the youngest children, and make it easier for an infant school to provide a suitable selection. Later on, when it comes to pens there will be other decisions. Should there be a free choice of modern or traditional pens? How early should children be allowed to use a pen? Left-handers will need special consideration. They profit from using pencils with leads that are not so hard as to dig into the paper, and from fibre-tipped pens that do not smudge. It is my experience that the more liberal a school policy is on such issues, the more the pupils will benefit. As in so many other matters, what suits one child may not suit another.

it makeS my riTiNG neeter

I Like the long felt tip

the pen be couse its comfortable to hold

and I can grip it Better.

becuase it is thin to writeR wim

it has a good nid

These eight-year-olds tried out ten different pens, and recorded their preferences.

The issue of lines sometimes causes heated discussion within or between schools, but the equally important issue of paper size seems seldom to be considered at all.

One seven-year-old boy proudly showed his school-made, scrap-book-sized handwriting book. When asked how he managed to reach the top lines where the text was written (the bottom half was reserved for illustrations), he described how 'of course' the chairs were too low to let him reach, so he lay flat on the table to write.

Large sheets of paper may be useful for free pre-writing pattern work or large directional exercises, but for the early skill lessons it is surely desirable to use small sheets of paper. A smaller size ensures that the child will never have to stretch too far to write. When emphasis is being put on an appropriate paper position a small sheet is an obvious advantage, particularly where table space is restricted. Half-sized exercise books that are then wider than long seem to work well.

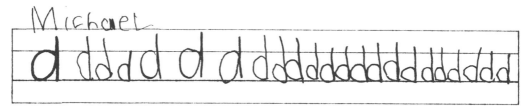

The letters in their own names usually indicate children's preferred size.

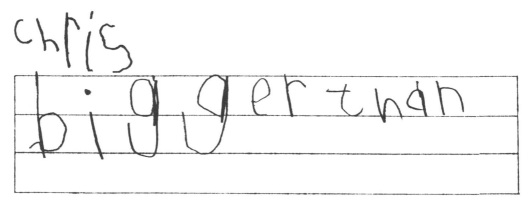

When lines are spaced too far apart they cause confusion.

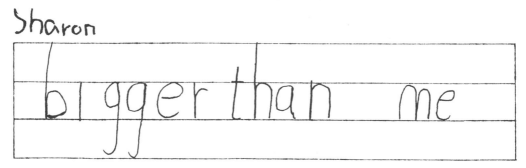

Widely spaced lines can lead to exaggerated ascending and descending strokes.

A teacher's quote: '*I have found it helps to give young children half-sized books when they are learning to write, especially those with a short concentration span as they are not put off by having a large page in front of them.*'

Lines are often a controversial issue. Some schools seem convinced that no children should have lines before the age of seven. Others set infants to write between four lines from the start. Surely either extreme is too inflexible. There may be some tasks that are best written on unlined paper and others where lines are a positive advantage. In the next section there are suggestions for staved training lines that are of particular help to children when they are trying to come to terms with height differentials. It is suggested that several sizes should be provided. Otherwise the choice of only one size per class means prescribing the size of writing within any particular group as soon as double lines are used. In some countries there are rigid rules about line spacing. The handwriting of all children of a certain age group is expected to be the same size. An interesting experiment that I carried out in Australia asked children about their preferred size of writing. Away from the classroom most of the children were able to reproduce almost exactly the size expected of them at school, but when asked what size they would like to write, the answers were usually quite different. It was not difficult to see the beneficial effects mirrored in their writing when they were able to choose the size.

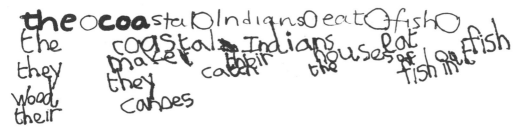

This example (reduced) shows a child in need of lines to help him keep his writing straight and make it legible.

A baseline, double lines or even four lines may be helpful at some time. A few years ago teachers from several schools involved in an inservice course undertook a small survey for me. They were all teaching infants in schools that did not approve of lines. All the children were asked to do some writing using paper with a baseline. Most of the children who had problems when writing on unlined paper showed improvement when given lines, but those who had mastered the difficult task of writing on unlined paper had problems using a baseline. A useful compromise is to try the lightly squared paper that is used in countries such as France and Spain. The unobtrusively checked background assists alignment without imposing size or slant on the writer. Teachers who have made small handwriting books out of squared paper have found it works well. The underlying message is that we need to have a more flexible and child-orientated attitude to so many matters concerning handwriting and that teachers should not be afraid to experiment. Children soon show us what works and what doesn't.

21 Making children aware of the importance of all these ideas

These sections have stressed how important it is for teachers to focus on practical issues. It is equally important that an awareness of these issues is transmitted to children. This can be done in several ways. When children are being given their first lessons in handwriting it is of course essential to teach good postural strategies, but unrealistic to expect this teaching to have much effect unless extra reminders are built into the teaching method. Ideally children need to internalise the feel of their optimum writing position. A little rhyme or poem made up each year with the new intake might serve as a first reminder. This could be repeated at the beginning of each skill session for the first few months. It could cover such matters as:

'I am sitting comfortably, not too high not too low.'
'My paper is to the side of my 'pencil hand.'
'I can see what I am doing (and the board).'
'I am holding my pencil so it can write well.'

Such an approach can be extended, for instance, to asking children if they can hear as well as see the teacher. In this way, potentially damaging conditions may be spotted early enough to be dealt with before they cause problems.

Children need space in order to write properly. When their desks get cluttered they contort themselves into incredible positions. This drawing is taken from an actual photograph, as are all the line drawings in this book.

Very young children can draw quite accurate pictures of good and bad posture.

In this way they may internalise the need to sit well.

A song rather than a poem might work well for a musical teacher, and the use of illustrations can be magical. Both younger and older children can be asked to draw pictures illustrating how to sit and how not to. The resulting pictures can be displayed and serve as a powerful reminder.

The aim is to make children aware of their own bodies and the part that handwriting posture plays in being able to work well. We want to educate children who are confident enough to say if their chairs or tables are not suitable, if they have not got enough space to work properly, if they cannot see or hear the teacher, and if they have not got a pencil that they find comfortable to use. Above all they must be encouraged to complain at the first signs of pain. It would be helpful if children were confident and informed enough to ask for lined paper if they felt that they needed it, and to be consulted about the size of the lines. It may not always be possible to provide each child's exact requirements but fostering this kind of awareness of preferences or potential problems, for both teachers and pupils, would be beneficial.

Using lines of different sizes and for different purposes

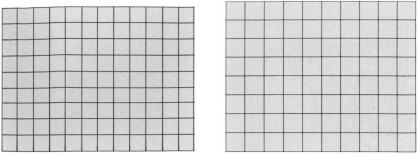

Squared paper gives guidance for alignment without imposing size.

Staved lines are ideal for teaching the heights of letters, but you will need several sizes to accomodate different children.

You can alternate a set of staved lines on a page with a baseline only, or you can highlight one or two lines with colour.

Imaginative use of lines from Norwegian copybooks by Moriggi and Arnesen (Aschehoug).

hk — ff —

Briem uses different weights of lines in his Icelandic copybooks.

PART 3

A system for teaching letters

This section provides a systematic method of teaching letters so that they move correctly and join naturally. It separates out those aspects of handwriting that need careful teaching from those that will develop naturally. A detailed explanation is given of the issues involved in joining. The aim is to provide you with a straightforward developmental teaching system that will cater for the needs of all children.

22 The vital early stages

Teachers who are informed and confident, using a system such as is proposed here, should be able to teach handwriting relatively easily providing enough time is given to skill training in the vital early days at school. The emphasis must be first on the movement of letters and the other concepts that lie behind our alphabet. These issues are more important than teaching children to follow the shape of the letters of models. Ideally teachers need a broader understanding of how handwriting works. This includes the realisation that letters are the visible trace of a hand movement so that the posture of the body also needs consideration.

Some children will need more reinforcement and encouragement than others in any or all of the aspects of writing, and undoubtedly a few children in every class may display real problems. If these problems persist despite a systematic approach and sympathetic and imaginative teaching, then they may indicate a need for special help. The sooner any physiological problems are diagnosed the better. However systematic it may be, a handwriting policy cannot cure all problems, but it may indicate them early on so that something can be done. This can prevent children in real difficulty from lagging too far behind the rest of the class.

The expectation must be that most pupils will not experience difficulties if they are taught systematically. For far too long the opposite has been the case. Most children are experiencing difficulty with handwriting because they have not had the essential skill training. When they are blamed for bad writing they start to become problems through no fault of their own. This starts a downward spiral of troubles. The children fall behind in written tasks and often become unwilling to put pen to paper. It is not an exaggeration to say that a whole generation has been labelled as poor writers. The cycle is complete when teachers who may not have learned good strategies themselves, much less had any training in how to teach handwriting, become convinced that handwriting is difficult both to teach and to learn.

This part of the book covers the early stages of teaching handwriting and provides flexible ideas within the systematic method proposed. It also suggests the value of observations and formal surveys. Such activities not only enable you to assess the effects of the school policy but also enlarge your own knowledge of the many issues involved in handwriting. A sequence of ideas is suggested but teachers are encouraged to expand and personalise their teaching in any way they feel appropriate. These strategies may mean a lot of work in the first year, but soon the new way of teaching and dealing with the movement of letters will become second nature. As the benefits spread upwards through the school it will all be worthwhile.

Ideas for the early lessons

These ideas are arranged in approximate sequence but no one other than the teacher on the spot can make the decison exactly how and when to start. The graphic development as well as the experience of young children can vary from one school to another, from one year's intake to the next as well as within each group. Some children may be used to sitting down and concentrating on a short task, while others may not be ready for some time. This is why each teacher must be the judge of exactly when to start the kind of programme that is suggested, within the structure of the school's own overall policy. To be too inflexible can be just as bad as having no system at all.

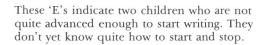

These 'E's indicate two children who are not quite advanced enough to start writing. They don't yet know quite how to start and stop.

To perceive and produce the difference between + and × is one indication of being ready to write.

The first lesson is very practical

The first 'proper' handwriting session can be made quite an occasion. First of all there are the practical points that need to be explained before the children are allowed to put pencil to paper:

Children are not all the same size at the same age. Appropriately-sized furniture is important when postural strategies are being formed. Chairs and tables of different sizes may look untidy but children's needs must come first at any age.

1. Their tables should be clear for the handwriting lesson.

2. They must be sitting comfortably.

3. They must choose a pencil, ideally from a selection of different sizes and shapes.

4. They must think about which of their hands will write best.

5. They need to be told that both hands have a job to do; one to hold the pencil and one to steady the paper.

6. They must put the paper a bit to the side of the hand that they are using to write with.

7. They might also be encouraged from the start to notice the shadow of their own hand. This way they become aware of the need for good lighting.

A teacher may need to repeat these instructions for quite a while, but there are entertaining ways of helping children to internalise the need for good writing posture. You can compose a song or rhyme, or better still the children can do it with you and perhaps incorporate their own terms. Later on it might be a good idea to see how far they understand it all. Why not ask them to draw a picture of someone sitting badly and well? That way the children's own pictures can reinforce your teaching. (See page 41.)

The matter of terminology has been discussed on pages 23–5 so it is sufficient to say here that whatever terms are decided should be used consistently.

23   The concepts behind our writing system

In order to teach handwriting confidently in the classroom, it is essential to be aware of the separate concepts that lie behind our alphabet and to be informed about methods of teaching each one. In fact the sequence is more-or-less the same for children: being aware, being taught strategies, and then becoming practised. These simple concepts are:

1.   The line of writing moves from left to right and top to bottom.

2.   Each letter has a prescribed movement and this is determined by the point of entry and direction of stroke.

3.   Height differentials are essential to the ultimate legibility of handwriting.

4.   Capital letters and small letters have their appropriate uses.

5.   Spacing, both of letters and words, is important.

6.   Several letters in our alphabet are mirror images of each other. (It is important that children are helped to form strategies for this difficult discrimination.)

Concept 1: The direction of writing

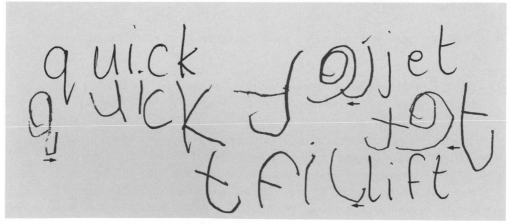

Young children often reverse the letters in their name or elsewhere. They start in the wrong place — at the end of a word or a line, and then proceed in the wrong direction.

Notice the reversals in the spelling corrections above. When writing from left to right letters often reverse automatically — try it yourself. All children need pre-writing exercises to automate a left-to- right direction. Some children need more reinforcement than others, left-handers usually even more than right-handers.

Concept 2: The movement of the strokes of individual letters

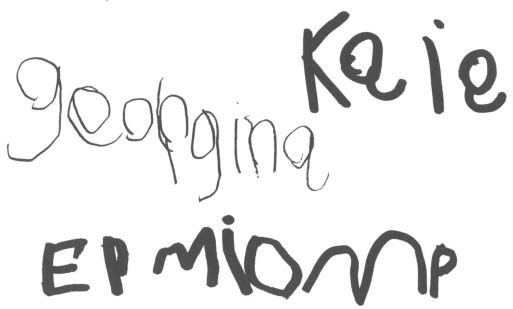

Children need to be taught the correct point of entry and direction of the strokes that make up each letter as soon as they begin to write as much as the letters of their own names. Letters are more easily taught and corrected in stroke-related groups than in alphabetical order.

Concept 3: Height differentials

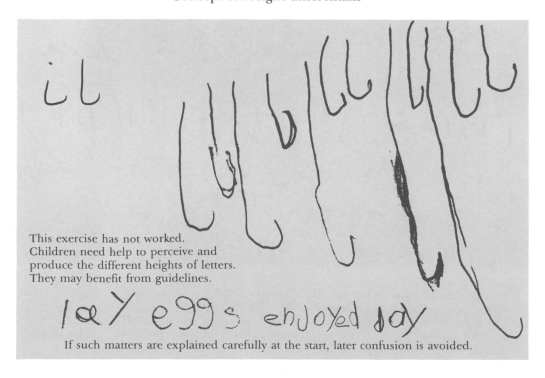

This exercise has not worked. Children need help to perceive and produce the different heights of letters. They may benefit from guidelines.

If such matters are explained carefully at the start, later confusion is avoided.

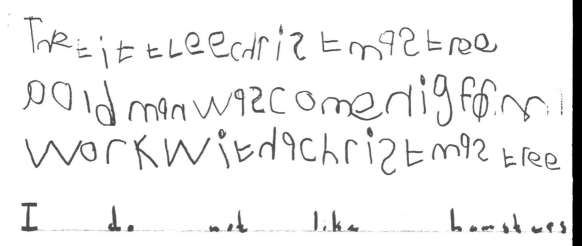

Young children need to be taught to allow spaces between words. It is not wise to teach them to use a thumb for word spacing, thumbs grow and letters get smaller. A space of one letter, usually an 'o' works much better when teaching children that words should neither run together nor be spaced too far apart.

Concept 5: Capital letters and small letters have different uses

Whatever explanation is used, it is important to set children on the right track or they may persist in using capital letters inappropriately, particularly when they are not concentrating. This happens frequently within names. Names are a good starting point . The specific use of an initial capital letter is an easy way of demonstrating the different functions of small and capital letters.

Ahdrew Ahbrew

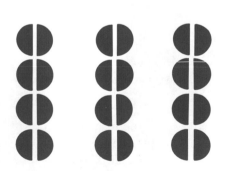

Pℕb ɪ Lⁱ∫ Pⁱzzp Pℕb

my bog is dlack

Our alphabet is designed from only a few strokes, so that several letters are mirror images of each other. Therefore specific reversals frequently occur. It is a particularly difficult for young children to discriminate between mirror images. Pre-writing exercises to promote mirror-image discrimination can help prevent reversals of letters.

Adults take all these separate aspects of the act of writing for granted but children need to be taught and to assimilate them separately. All these logical steps must be taken one-by-one before a child is ready to put them together and write.

When teachers are aware of the importance of these steps it is then a matter of finding an explicit way of dealing with the issues one-by-one. Experienced teachers have their own effective ways of doing things, and may just want to have the help of a sequence to support them. The ideas in this part of the book are intended to stimulate teachers' imaginations to make this first vital stage of learning purposeful, as well as lively and fun. Your own ideas about terminology may well be more valuable than those suggested here, the children's contributions may be even better.

b | d
—————
p | q

Exercises like these help develop mirror-image discrimination. Use any material you like for matching, pairing up and making patterns with semicircles.

A diagram like this is another simple way of demonstrating letters that are almost mirror images of each other.

24 Different approaches to teaching

Children learn in different ways, some take in visual information best, some need extra kinaesthetic feedback while others need actions to be described orally. The third category of children is perhaps the most difficult to satisfy in the classroom. It is not easy for adults to describe the separate steps of an action that they perform automatically. To be sure that all children understand what is being taught in the early stages of writing, all three of these methods should be employed. A certain amount of repetition or reinforcement will be beneficial, and might be vital to the few children who initially learn only in one of the three ways.

With handwriting it is widely recognised that kinaesthetic feedback is essential; because handwriting is a motor skill it does not and should not depend exclusively on visual feedback. Some of the movement training for handwriting should be carried out with the eyes shut to help children internalise the movement of letters.

Teacher's remark: *'Teaching handwriting involves a lot of talking.'*
(This particular teacher evolved an imaginative vocabulary to talk pre-school children through the movement of each letter.)

Three ways of teaching movement illustrated by 'k'

Icelandic children using Briem's method learn that 'k' is like a sack tied in the middle.

Næstur er stafurinn k.
Hann er eins og h með
hart gyrta beltisól.

This lovely example explains the relationship between the letters 'h' and 'k'. It says that 'k' is like an 'h' with a tight belt on. From Italiu-skrift, a handwriting scheme for Iceland by G. SE Briem, 1988.

Nan Barchowsky's children in USA write their letter 'k' to the instruction 'down up and over, tuck it in kick it out'. Australian children might approve of the method I saw in quite another country – a cut-out kangaroo with the letter 'k' on it. The letter was made of beans stuck on a 'k' shape that had previously been written with a brush in glue. Many materials from glitter to rice, sand or feathers can be used to decorate 'glue' letters. (Smarties used to mark their initials on small iced cakes were a popular variation of this technique with my own three children.)

25 Explaining the act of writing in a logical sequence

The whole purpose of handwriting is that it should be automatic so that fluent writers can forget about their hands and concentrate on the content of their writing. For this reason adults may not realise how many essential sub-tasks are involved in producing letters. Handwriting is a taught skill, and nothing about it comes naturally. It may take a real effort to sort out the logical sequence of actions in order to explain them to children, but this is essential, because the early lessons in the movement of strokes and then of letters are vital. The first lesson about the movement of writing could go something like this:

1. Explain to the children that writing is a bit different to drawing, and that they have got to teach their pencils to do what they are told.

2. They must teach the pencil to go from left to right and from the top of the page downwards. If you adopt the kind of idea on page 71 you can say 'start on the side with the tall boy, girl, clown or whatever, and always start at the head'.

3. Explain to the children that letters are just a pattern of different strokes and that they are going to start with a pattern that works in the same way as handwriting. At some stage you will have to explain that the letters that you are aiming at are not capital letters, but small friendly ones that run along the line easily and quickly. Start with a scallop pattern which can be described as scoops or waves. Demonstrate this in the air and on the board before everyone has a try. Watching children producing even this simple pattern will give you a good idea of which ones are going to have difficulties with letters.

Many simple materials can be used in imaginative ways at the pre-writing or early stages of teaching writing. Trays with sand or salt, or finger paint are useful and fun for practising pattern, strokes or letters. Small individual slates which were once the most usual way of practising writing can still be used. They correspond to the blackboard and can be a constructive as well as a cheap and permanent tool in the classroom.

4. Tell children that some letters are tall and some are short. Alter the scallop pattern to include tall and short lines. You should reinforce the tall/short principle with other ideas in whatever materials are available in the classroom.

Teacher's idea: 'To demonstrate heights on the blackboard, a music ruler can be used with different coloured chalks to accentuate the difference between the heights.'

5. Explain that all letters start at the top (except 'e' and 'd' which will be taught later). The top to you may be the top of the board as you write downwards. To children the 'top' is actually the point furthest away from their body and the bottom is the point nearest to them. You can demonstrate the 'starting at the top'

idea to children by rolling a small ball or marble towards them on their desk. A miniature model car or bus is also useful for demonstrating the trajectory of letters in a way that is immediately obvious to children. Remember that it is difficult for some children to relate one plane to another so do not expect all your class to be able to pick up points made on the blackboard. Most children need the reinforcement of seeing each of the early stages of writing reproduced individually for them on their own paper. This may be time consuming, and difficult to organise but it will pay off in the end. Left-handers will profit from a demonstration by the teacher with the left hand. If the resulting handwriting is not perfect this does not matter. The important thing is that the children should assimilate the correct movement in the easiest possible way.

At this stage the movement of letters can be internalised in many different ways using a variety of media.

Teachers idea: 'Write the letter in chalk on the blackboard and let the child rub it out to learn movement.' (This works even better on a small slate.)

These traditional Chinese methods can be adapted: a thick red letter for the child to write over, or an outlined letter with the start and the order of the strokes indicated.

Letters made from rolled plasticine, clay or baked dough provide a three dimensional approach to letters. They can be cheaply and easily made at home or school, as can letters made out of furry material or sandpaper for kinaesthetic reinforcement. Inscribed letters can be made out of anything from wood and hardened clay to soap or chocolate. Children might find them easier to scoop out of softer materials such as dough, cake icing or even ice-cream. This stage can be great fun for children and adults alike.

Design student's idea: 'Some years ago I was helping a post-graduate student with her project; designing aids for teaching handwriting skills to pre-school children. She had produced some interesting flexible wire letters that exactly reproduced the movement of letters, and would be more durable than plasticine, clay or baked dough. They needed a finishing touch so I suggested painting them to look like snakes and giving them a red tongue to indicate the point of entry.'

26 Introducing letters in stroke related families

By separating letters into groups that use the same strokes, teaching the movement of letters becomes more effective. The hand then practises sequences that repeat and reinforce each movement in such a way that it soon becomes automated. To encourage this automation process each small sequence can be practised at speed as soon as possible. Of course at this stage one-to-one supervision is specially needed to ensure that correct rather than incorrect movement is being automated.

The four families of letters

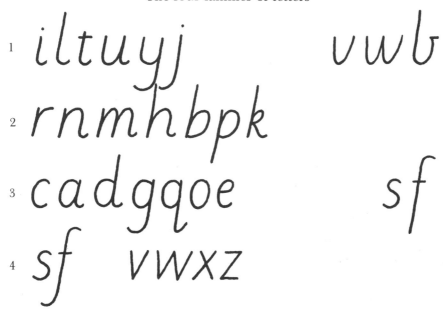

The letters of the alphabet separated into stroke related groups. Notice how the rounded 'v' and 'w' and an undercurve 'b' would change their group. The letters 's' and 'f' could go with either the 'c' family because they share the same point of entry, or with the diagonal and complex letters because they involve a change of direction.

Marking point of entry on letters

There are no indications of the point of entry on the letter sequences in this book. This is not because they are unnecessary, rather to the contrary. When everything is pre-prepared and given out on sheets to young children there is always a risk of details being taken for granted. Maybe children should be involved in the marking of the point of entry on their own sheets, and then there would be a real understanding of the purpose. Pupils could choose which colour to use, and the whole issue made into a positive experience that might fix the importance of the point of entry more firmly in each child's mind. If any teachers disagree with this or feel that it is too much to expect of young children, then they may have to indicate the point of entry on individual photocopied desk strips, because undoubtedly this is better when done in a bright contrasting colour.

27 Teaching the first letter family

When you think that most children are ready, introduce the letters 'i,l,t' using the same terminology that you used for patterns, but stressing always that each letter starts at the top or head. If you are going to use letters with exit strokes then you will need a word to describe the upstroke. Your children might enjoy deciding for you. Some of the words that teachers use are 'tail', 'flick', 'kick', '...and up', or even 'curl'.

If you prefer you can introduce the letters two at a time, starting with 'i,l'. You would not want to concentrate on a single letter for too long because the different heights are essential comparisons from the start. Make sure that somehow you watch each child to check that they are producing the correct movement. These first steps are the most vital ones. You will have to spend extra time with those who arrived at school already forming letters from the base upwards.

Are you wondering what to do about the dot on the 'i', and the cross on the 't'? The letter 't' is special in two ways: it is a different height from other letters and it has a crossbar. Both of these factors need to be explained carefully and then to be practised. You could leave the dot out for the first day if you wanted to concentrate on the different heights of the three letters. When you teach the second set in the family; 'u,y,j', the dots can be a lesson on their own. They can be used to show how important it is to be able to tell the difference between one letter and another – between 'i' and 'l' (as that is all that they have been taught) and 'i,j' and 'y'. Combine this with the crossbar and the height of letters and you have the opportunity for explaining in very simple terms the importance of legibility and the uses of writing. In other words you can see that other people need to read what you have written.

Teacher's idea: 'To help children remember that there are three different heights of letter and that 't' is the only mid-height letter; call the letter 't' a teenager.'

When most of the children have mastered these three letters you could reward them with some words; 'it', 'ill', 'lit'. Ideally no child should progress to the next family of letters before they are confident about the movement of the previous one. This may sound didactic but it is the only way of making sure that pre-school errors are corrected at the first possible moment and that children are set on the right path to basic letters with a correct movement.

Each school will have to decide whether to encourage pupils to keep examples of their work in a folder, so that everyone is able to chart their own progress. Another feature could be to teach self-criticism – perhaps self-appraisal is a better word – in a gentle way. Some schools manage to do this within the whole class by getting several children at a time to write whatever is the current exercise on the blackboard. Then they look for the good or best points in each one. It must be done in a positive way – never competitively or in a 'looking for bad points' atmosphere. It is always possible to find something good in a piece of writing.

il il il ilt ilt ilt itu itu

---

uy uy uy uyj uyj uyj

---

iltilt ill lit till lit tilt

The first family of letters is made up of downstrokes leading to under-arches. Various sequences are shown here printed in 'Sassoon Primary', a typeface designed to bridge the gap between letters for reading and letters for writing.

Suitable letter sequences for handwriting practice need thought, as does the method of reproducing them. Many teachers will write out appropriate exercises in individual books. Others may like to cut up copies of the sequences on pages 6–9. In time letters and words generated on the school computer may provide exercise material. The typeface shown here, 'Sassoon Primary' has been designed for this purpose. It is a clear, legible typeface for use in producing reading material for young children and for printing out letter sequences or handwriting exercises. This typeface incorporates exit strokes at the baseline, which bond letters together to accentuate the word shape for young readers. The exit strokes also provide a link between the letters for reading and the suggested way of teaching the first stages of handwriting. The typeface does not pretend to be handwriting or a handwriting model in the traditional sense, but purposely there is enough suggestion of move-ment in the letters for children to see how handwriting works.

The prospect of producing flexible exercises, that could be stored on a disc and printed as required to fit with a school's policy, is exciting. It could mean the end of expensive copybooks, and the opportunity to match exercises to the needs of individual children.

28 Teaching the second letter family

You can use an over-curve pattern to introduce the next family of letters: 'h,n,m,r', 'p,b,k'. Once again children can be encouraged to put a coloured mark at the point of entry, the top, of their personal desk strip. Some children profit from exercises where instead of being expected to produce a line of spontaneous letters, certain parts of each letter are indicated. They are helped to an understanding of the correct movement by being left to fill in the gaps before they are expected to produce complete letters. You can break up most letters into their component strokes if necessary, using either solid or dotted lines. The ideas on page 72 are also appropriate.

The letters in this family divide into two logical sets, but you can introduce them to your children in pairs or as you think fit. There are many explicit ways of describing the differences between letters in the same group. For example you can say that 'h' goes down up and over and 'n' is just a short 'h', 'm' is like a double 'n' and 'r' is just half an 'n'. The letters can be superimposed on each other in different colours to highlight similarities and differences. A base line may help with ascenders and descenders or a block of colour for the body of the letter and lines for the ascenders and descenders. It is easy to think up imaginative ways of presenting letter families to make this stage of learning interesting and effective.

When these letters are mastered you have a considerable repertoire of letters to use for simple words. If you think some of your pupils are getting impatient you can construct simple phrases like 'in my hut' or 'it hit him' using only the first two families. If most of your pupils are absolute beginners it may be better to continue with the systematic teaching of letters until all the four families have been mastered. That will be for you to decide. It is also up to you whether you want to use some simple checklist or merit star system to make sure that each family of letters has been successfully learned. A similar check might be useful at intervals later on to make sure that no one is slipping back into movement faults as they start to write words and sentences.

mn hr rnmhbpk

The second family of letters comprises those with over-arches.

bpk bpk bpk

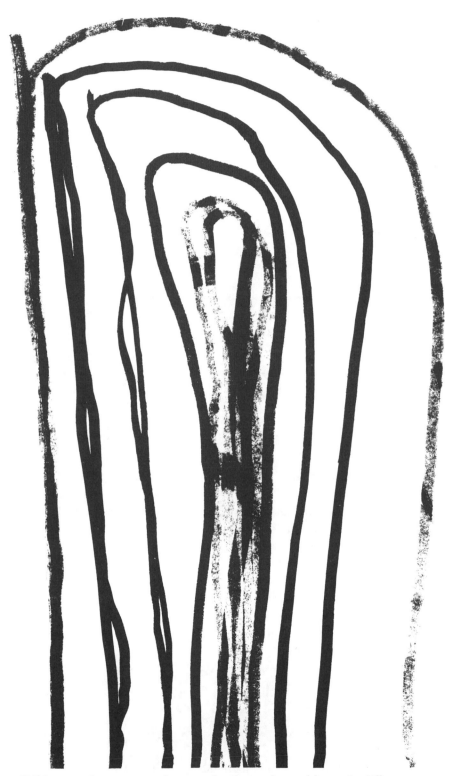

Children can be encouraged to practise the strokes and letters in different ways.

29 Teaching the round letters

The next family of letters are based on the letter 'c'. Once the correct point of entry to this letter is established the letters 'a,d,g,q,o' and perhaps 'e' can easily be taught together. Some of the letters are slightly more complex, involving a change of direction. This may be difficult for those children who are not as graphically advanced as their peers.

acacac cad cad cad

---

cc cco cco cdg cdg

The third family of letters could be termed 'round'. They are based on the letter 'c'.

The round group of letters may need to be taught more slowly than the previous two, with more repetition of sequences and frequent talking through of the movement of the letters as well as plenty of kinaesthetic reinforcment. If a teacher is musical the 'round about and up and downness' of this family of letters can be helped by setting it to music. The letter 'e' can come into this group with emphasis put onto the 'further round' point of entry.

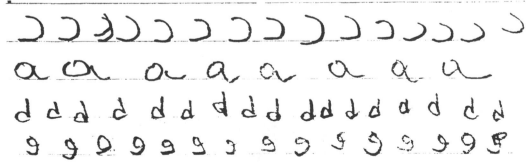

Exercises based on letter families do more harm than good if the basic movement is not correct. Individual supervision is needed at the beginning.

30 Complex letters and emerging problems

By this stage the children will have learned the three straightforward families of letters: those with downstrokes, those with under- or over-curves, and the group related to the letter 'c'. The fourth group of letters contain those that sometimes prove difficult: those with diagonal strokes and the letters 's', 'f' and 'k' that involve changes of direction.

At some stage you will need to find out whether each child is able to perceive and produce all the strokes that make up our letters. The most difficult are often the diagonal strokes. A zigzag pattern will help you to see those children who may find the traditional zigzag 'w' troublesome. Some young children may find it difficult to differentiate between '+' and '×', so some letters may be a problem for them. Patterns such as superimposed '×' and '+' can be used as a help in diagnosing potential difficulties. The same patterns can then be used to help young children to learn how to deal with the problem if it is only a matter of delayed graphic ability. More serious conditions may mean that children continue to have difficulties with certain strokes. In that case observant teachers can be instrumental in reporting such difficulties so that early diagnosis and extra help can be provided.

This is the time to decide whether to try some of the alternative letterforms provided with the model alphabets. Children in difficulty could be offered the alternative 'v' and 'w' with a scooped under-curve, or the chance to choose which form of the letter 'k' they find easiest.

$$kkkk \quad vwxz \quad vow$$

$$ok \ ok \quad vwxz \quad vow$$

The fourth group of letters have diagonal strokes, which some children find difficult. If so, a rounded 'v' or 'w' can help. Several alternatives are provided for 'k'. The letters 's' and 'f' can be included in this group, being complex letters, or they can be taught with the group on the opposite page, because they have a similar 'top-right' point of entry.

Letters that involve changes of direction are a considerable manupulative task for untrained or clumsy hands.The letters 's' and 'f' are often difficult initially for left-handers. Those who find such difficulties often show their problems by enlarging the letters that they find difficult. All they are doing is indicating that their hands need a bit more space in which to manoeuvre. Instead of criticising such children for uneven writing, understanding teachers can help by letting children experiment with simplified forms of the problem letters as soon as possible.

31 Name writing

So far it has been suggested that the first teaching of letters should be carried out in stroke-related families, but there is another aspect of early writing that deserves attention. That is the question of how children write their names. Many children will have made an attempt at name writing before they come to school. Whether parents or older brothers and sisters have helped them, or whether they have picked it up themselves it is quite likely that there are movement faults in these early letters. The child's name is so often written during the school day that it is suggested that name writing should be incorporated into early skill training sessions. It is essential to teach or correct the movement of letters within each child's name before an incorrect movement becomes automated. If this is done early enough and thoroughly enough, much of the correction of pre-school errors can be dealt with. The use of capital letters can be explained at the same time in the context of name writing. Criticism of anything learned at home, or anything as personal as a name must be sensitively handled. In terms of efficient teaching, a combination of letter families and name writing may be the most effective and time-saving way of covering the teaching of the essential movement of letters.

Add a self portrait to a name and you have a doubly useful tool for diagnosis. These were some of the least mature drawings and letters from a pre-school class of Australian five-year-olds. A lot of work would be needed to prevent movement and other faults in these names from becoming automated.

Names again become an issue when children join without knowing how.

60

Correcting the letters in a child's name in three stages

Michael came to school with several movement faults in his name. The first step was to use the 'c' to teach the letter 'a'.

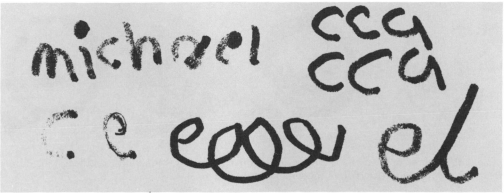

In the second session, the 'h' was added. More work was needed on 'a', this time by comparing 'a' to 'e'.

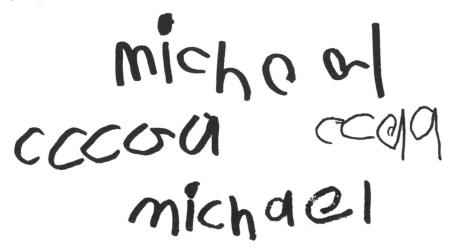

A further attack on 'a' and success at last in the third session but reinforcement still needed.

32 Designing exercises

It is at this stage that many handwriting schemes provide a variety of photocopiable material to hand out for general use in class. While this is of obvious advantage to the busy teacher, it has to be questioned whether this is to the benefit of many of the children. All too often a standard exercise is offered to all the children, whether they are already practised in that particular exercise or not yet ready for it. This book does not pretend to be a handwriting scheme. It is a progression of ideas for the teaching of handwriting, and one of its aims is to help teachers to understand each stage in such a way that they are always aware of the differing levels and needs of their group of pupils. If your school has any photocopiable exercises use them as you think fit, but remember that it is not the exercise alone that is going to be of help. The teacher is the vital link. It is the selection of something that suits the child, plus the supervision of the exercise to make sure that its particular lesson is being followed, that really helps.

The child who completed this exercise on the formation of 'Q' may have had fun, but did not learn anything about the correct movement of the letter.

There is another point; if you have used any of the ideas concerning variations of slant, proportion, alternative letterforms or different sizes and lines, standard exercises become a bit of a contradiction of concept. A few schools have tried out the techniques suggested in this book over a period of several years and their comments are likely to be more useful than any more theoretical paragraphs. Most children are likely to be given a personal handwriting exercise book. The format suggested by all of the teachers who were consulted, was approximately A5, used horizontally. Some teachers used squared paper, some paper with a baseline only and some experimented with staved lines. They allowed for four or five repetitions of any exercise to appear on the page. This satisfies the criteria of allowing a certain amount of repetition but not too much. More than four repetitions demonstrated a deterioration as the child either got bored or too far from the 'model' of the exercise that the teacher had written. Most of the teachers involved set a short time at the beginning of each school day for formal handwriting practice. The teachers set the day's exercise either individually or in preselected groups of children, and they usually prepared these exercises the evening before. A system for doing this at the beginning or during the session could be organised if desired.

Exercises should be tailored to children's needs, sensibly supervised and corrected

Approval of this copying would only confirm the incorrect movements.

Specific help with movement and heights is needed before more copying.

The rhyme, 'Mike Moose are millions of Mars bars', was meant for practising the letters 'm' and 'o', but as each of the circles (and 'o's) started at the baseline it was not helpful.

Sequences like 'adad' or 'adg' would teach more than repeating a single letter.

Maybe the enthusiasm for this method carried the teachers over the first, time-consuming weeks, but they professed to be delighted with the results and realised that with time the preparation of such exercises would become far easier and quicker. One school has now been doing this for four years, and although it is the reception teacher who has done most of the work, the benefits reported from the junior school make it all worthwhile. The flexibility of this system can be illustrated here by one or two examples and the teacher's remarks about her system..

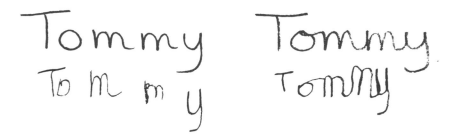

Teacher's comment: 'I always start with the letters in a child's name'.

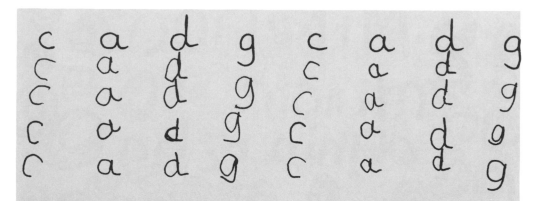

Next come repetitive exercises in family groups. These are done in small booklets on lined paper, or better still, on square paper.

This method soon leads on to short words as each group of letters is assimilated. Do not expect perfect letters; the object is to teach the correct movement. These come from five-year-olds in their first weeks of schooling, but notice how 'mum' is already beginning to join. That is the result of teaching letters with exit strokes.

33 Starting to use letters

Once children are confirmed in the correct movement of letters they are ready to use them. If this has been systematically planned, and confidently taught it should not have taken too long. How and when children are encouraged to try to put down their thoughts on paper must be a whole school decision, fitting in with spelling and other policies. The standard of handwriting will inevitably decline once other learned skills such as spelling are combined with the simple production of letters. It may have been possible to get most of a class to produce the letter families in exercise form to a relatively high level of competence. At the next stage common combinations of letters or a few short words combining the different groups of letters can be given to young children to copy. Even this is enough to disrupt the smooth production of letters. Put it another way: if letters are taught in stroke related groups because this is the easiest way to assimilate them, it stands to reason that even mixing all the letters of the alphabet up, is likely to be slightly more difficult.

The copying of a sentence under a picture might be the next stage. This would involve yet another problem: word spacing. The final stage in this short progression might be where a child attempts to spell as well as write down letters. As more tasks are loaded onto children their concentration on the formation of letters is diminished. It may be necessary to consider whether reinforcement is needed to ensure that all the good work that has been put into the training of the movement of letters is not being endangered. Teachers need to look for indications that children are not being hurried along too fast, nor on the other hand being held back. It is a difficult balance to maintain, and one where there can be no set rules.

Teachers comment: 'Every day I prepare an exercise for every child'.

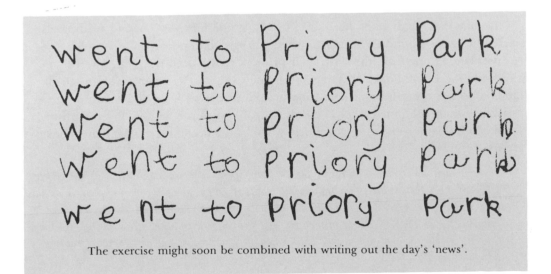

The exercise might soon be combined with writing out the day's 'news'.

After a certain stage it would be possible to cut the teacher's preparation time by letting the more competent pupils copy the day's exercise from the blackboard. This would still allow enough flexibility to deal with the small proportion of children with specific problems who would, for instance, be needing more reinforcement of the movement of basic letters. Several more old-fashioned schools have reported to have followed similar systems for years. Some continue the 'daily exercises' on into junior school, but for how long this is done must be a decision for each school.

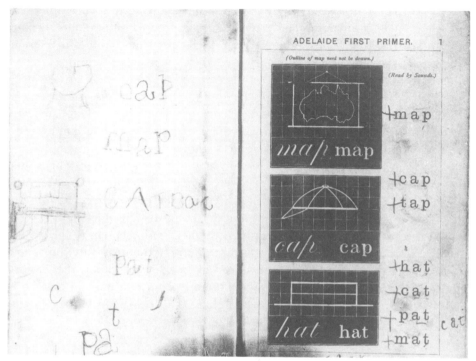

This nineteenth century Australian primer showed the written letterforms but the child chose to copy the printed ones.

The way that handwritten letters can be integrated into spelling and reading also needs thought. A hundred years ago when young children learned a complex copperplate writing from the start, their primers reproduced the written word alongside the printed one. This may not be necessary today when children see all kinds of letters reproduced as television graphics or advertising and seem to assimilate them all quite easily. The difference between the written and the printed word can be demonstrated to advantage when popular commercial sentence-makers are used in class.

A teacher's idea about how to integrate the popular typeset sentence-makers into a handwriting scheme: 'Let the children pick the typeset words as supplied by the manufacturers as this part is letter recognition and should tie up with reading. Each word should, however, be handwritten on the reverse side of the card and the children trained to reverse the card when they fit it into the sentence frame. Then when they write the sentence, they are copying handwriting not type.'

34 Lines

Most infant schools will use unlined paper for these early lessons, although increasingly they are considering the advantages of baselines for some written tasks from the beginning. It is soon possible to spot those children who find difficulty in judging the different heights of letters. These are the ones who may need special lines, maybe two or even three or four, to help them to sort out the ascending and descending strokes even during the introduction to letter families.

A New York teacher's names for the four lines, two red and two blue, that she used for teaching height differentials: 'The living room carpet, the living room ceiling, the basement and the attic roof.' She demonstrated this on the blackboard with coloured chalks.

Where there is a liberal policy on lines, or no lines used at all, it will become evident that children soon settle down to what might be termed their optimum writing size. This will differ from child to child, so it may not be a good idea to do anything that imposes just one size of writing on a whole group of children. This means that as soon as a teacher considers that double lines are a good idea for any purpose, it is desirable to have several sets of such lines to suit different sizes of writing. It is necessary to go a little deeper into the reasons behind different sizes of writing. Tension can affect the size of handwriting from a surprisingly early age, causing small or even minute letters. On the other hand, clumsy hands may prevent certain children from performing the strokes of the more complex letters in as small an area as other children are able to do. Trying to regulate either of these conditions by using one standard set of lines is unlikely to be successful.

It is with this in mind that these sets of staved teaching lines are suggested. They can be enlarged or reduced on a photocopier and arranged in several sets on a page for specific practice work. Ideally they should be used on small sheets of not more than four or five sets. They are most useful with the youngest age groups, because once staved lines are reduced beyond a certain size, the staves and the spaces between sets become muddled. A few schools use spaced out staved lines like these for general writing purposes in the early years. This may make children's work easy to read but it uses rather a lot of paper. In addition it might lead children to think that all writing has to be line-spaced in order to be legible.

Sets of staved lines are useful when the heights of letters are being taught, but several different sizes should be provided. (See page 42.)

35 Drawing with writing

One of the pilot schools that followed the teaching system outlined here, reported towards the end of the first year that the standard of the children's drawing was noticeably higher than it had been in previous intakes. This showed in two ways. The children were observing details of objects that they portrayed. In the case of this particular school, which was involved in a project on the history of their village, pictures on the walls portrayed complicated subjects such as sewing machines in considerable detail. Moreover the line quality and precision of the actual drawings certainly seemed of a very high quality for such young children. The class teacher explained both of these factors as results of the children's observation and production of letter details such as careful exit strokes, plus the precision developed by the five- and six-year-olds during the early teaching of joined letters.

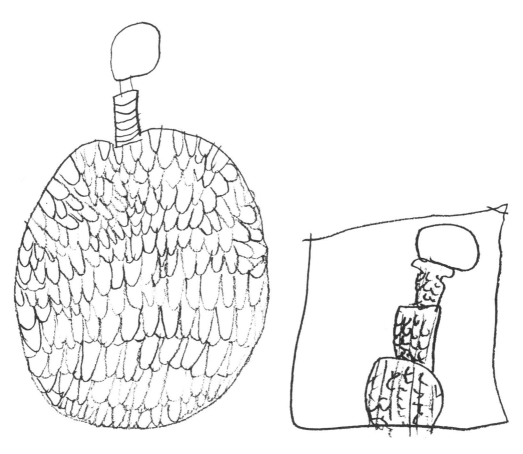

These drawings of a perfume bottle were produced by two children in their first year of school. The picture opposite was produced by a child of similar age in another school.

Observational drawing can help towards the specific skills needed for handwriting. The reverse is also true: the careful observation and production of letters in a systematic teaching method can result in an interesting increase in detail and quality in young children's drawings.

Some time later I was shown two projects in the north of England, both of which involved developing children's powers of artistry and expressive language through direct observational drawing. The schools had found that one of the additional benefits of such a programme was the development of motor skills necessary for the promotion of fluent handwriting.

Whether schools wish to follow a positive policy of observational drawing, or whether they are happy to let children's drawings develop in a more detailed way as a result of closer and more careful teaching of the details of letters, there is a lesson to be learned from these two projects. Few young children are given opportunities to exercise detailed discrimination in tasks such as purposeful observational drawing or training in the details of letters. The results of years of leaving children to develop their own handwriting have shown that such discrimination and accurate production of detail do not come naturally to other than a very few talented children. Like so many other things, these skills need to be developed and can be taught imaginatively.

36 Remedial work often begins on day one

As most experienced teachers know, many children start school with bad habits that need correcting. Then there are those children who find it more difficult than others to assimilate the early lessons for whatever reason. A third group of children that may need considerable remedial help are those who may have moved to the school from another district where such intensive early training has not been carried out. All these children will need systematic help to correct their movement and other faults as soon as they are recognised. Although there may be special circumstances such as individual children's need to settle in to a new environment, in general the longer such faults are left the harder they are to alter. In the children's own interest it is important to take action as soon as possible, although considerable tact may be necessary on the part of the teacher when dealing both with children and parents. The remedial techniques suggested here would have to be combined with any necessary help in dealing with postural problems.

To understand their difficulties you need to watch children in action as well as to scrutinise their letters.

A good way of setting about pinpointing handwriting faults is to run through the six concepts on pages 46–9, bearing in mind these questions:

1. Are directional problems noticeable either from the letters or the child's actions when writing?

2. Do all the letters move correctly, with the strokes starting at the correct point and moving in the right direction?

3. Does it appear that the child understands about the different heights of letters?

4. What about capital letters? Does the child use them in a way that shows appropriate use of the different levels of letters?

5. Are letters and words spaced in a way that shows understanding of inter-letter and inter-word spacing?

6. Are there reversals, either simple ones such as b/d mirror images or more complex one involving letters that are upside down as well as mirrored?

Maybe you have a whole new class displaying a variety of handwriting problems. Where should you start? Only you can tell where most difficulties lie, and problems may differ from intake to intake. A practical suggestion is to take a sample of writing from everyone in the group. Look quickly through the examples and sort them into piles of those displaying each of the six problems highlighted above. In all probability the largest proportion of children will display movement faults. A further look will show you which family of letters is causing the most problem. Suppose it is the family that includes 'a', 'd' and 'g'. That becomes your starting point for a whole-class remedial lesson.

Ideas for helping with directional problems

Nothing about handwriting is natural; everything needs to be taught. In other cultures writing moves from right to left, which might make it easier for left-handers who may need more reinforcement in a left-to-right movement in the early stages. They may profit from a reminder in their writing books for a while. A strip of red paper or plastic clipped to the left edge is a good idea. The clown strip supplied by 9-year-old Sophie Lovett, and a younger child's pen portrait are even more fun. These techniques emphasise the possible benefits of first explaining and then involving each child in an imaginative way, in solving the problems of automating each of the necessary 'rules' of writing.

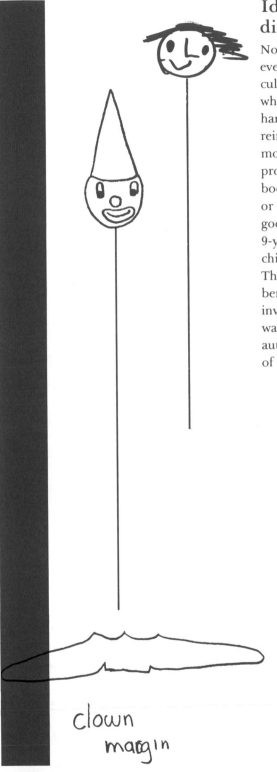

clown
margin

Dealing with movement problems

There is no single magic exercise to alter the incorrect movement of letters. It is essential to find something that each child relates to. Try using an overhead projector. This gives a three dimensional effect to the movement of letters and children enjoy it. Use the face of the clock to teach the point of entry (providing the child can tell the time). A model car or animal on wheels can demonstrate the trajectory of letters, while the teacher talks through the movement. Ensure that you use appropriate repetitive sequences of letters. It may be necessary to separate the strokes of complex letters to show children how they fit together, and then to follow this up with partial dotting or shading in of letters to support the early stages of retraining. Use your imagination and make it all light-hearted.

You can cut simple letters out of cardboard or a textured material such as sandpaper. These will provide children with stencils to write in or feel around, and solid letters to handle.

You can use a thick colour marker pen or a graphite block to write a letter, letting children watch the movement and then write over.

A piece of string can be used to demonstrate the unnecessary extra movement that is often made on the letter 'f'. Follow this up with a sequence that ties the point of entry to that of 'c' and 's'.

The solutions suggested in this chapter have all been visual or tactile ones. It is important to remember that it is the hand itself that has to be retrained. We often say that all letters should start at the top (except 'e' and 'd'). Therefore, if may be helpful if you explain to children to start by pulling their letters towards themselves, not by pushing away. Remember that children can become confused if you always refer to up and down movements, when on the flat plane of their table, writing movements are actually nearer or further away from their bodies.

Helping with height differentials

Height differentials can be talked through, and then demonstrated by writing on the board between different coloured lines. Similar sets of lines can then be used in individual exercises to help those who have difficulty in assimilating this concept. Another way of explaining is to use long and short wooden rods that can be handled. Young children might enjoy pacing or skipping on the floor over chalk letters so that they can experience the combined downward movement of letters and the variable lengths. Children will vary in how they relate to the different techniques; an observant teacher will soon notice which approach is suitable.

boy

Underline to accentuate baseline.

buy

Accentuating word shape.

hill

Accentuating ascenders.

jig

Accentuating descenders.

bag

pool

Two ways of accentuating x-height letters.

There will probably be plenty of other minor imperfections in young children's writing. Letters may differ to a certain extent in size and slant, but you need to deal with important principles first. Each child, however old, will need to be taken back as far as is necessary, maybe right back to basic letter families, so that you can explain and demonstrate each principle that is not yet clearly understood.

Reminders will need to be given frequently, particularly with movement problems. This could be at the end of written work, in the same way as you might give spelling corrections. This is not repressive. It is far worse to allow significant faults to continue once children are in a formal teaching situation. You would then be in the position of giving your tacit approval to an error that will eventually have to be tackled, with potentially far greater inconvenience to the pupil and all concerned.

Capital letters

Children need a clear explanation of the usage of capital letters and the ways in which they differ from small letters. This should be done as early as possible because once confusion sets in over capital letters, they can become a focus of tension. A simple exercise using the children's names might help. Choose a name that starts with whichever letter a particular child has problems, for example Martin for capital 'M'; not Sam, Rose for capital 'R', but not Mary. Another way could be to use solid or overprinted letters for comparison, such as those on page 00. Be sure to point out the possible change in movement between such pairs as 'M' and 'm', and 'N' and 'n'. Lines may help in stressing that 'Oo', 'Ss', 'Cc' and 'Pp', for example, differ only in size.

'Spacing problems'

Once children are taught that a word space should be approximately the size of a letter 'o', and not a finger space, there should be less confusion. The concept of word spacing can be demonstrated with different coloured plastic letters so the space can be felt as well as seen. Letter spacing will improve once exit strokes are included from the start. Good spacing of words or letters is dependent on being able to see what has been written. Left-handers may need to alter their paper position to clear the line of vision, and some poor spacing may signal the need for an eye test. Uneven spacing can also be caused by tension, too much downward pressure so the hand jerks along, or a misguided idea that writing is easier to read if it is widely spaced.

Reversals and mirror images

Children who are experiencing difficulty in discriminating between mirror images often like to have some kind of visual or aural reminder. Try tying 'd' to the related letter 'a' by suggesting 'adadad' as a pattern, then using the word 'add' or 'dad' as a reminder. This adds a phonic element to the reminder. In the same way 'b' gets associated to 'p' in a 'bpbpbp' pattern, and the word 'pub' can be used as a reminder.

A dyspraxic child's solution to his b/d problem: overprinting 'dag' and 'pb' to make two patterns. One he called 'dag' and the other 'pobble' – his names, not mine – and this method worked for him.

Many reversal problems should never arise if the systematic method of teaching suggested in this book is used. If the movement is stressed as much or even more than the visual resemblances between the sets of letters, this will help those children who might be most prone to muddle them.

ɓad   **bad**

Another suggestion is to use an under-curve 'b' that is less like a mirror image of d'.

When the movement of letters is discussed, 'd' is described as the only letter (other than 'e') that starts in the middle. It begins like 'a' and then goes right up and down. The letter 'b' on the other hand, is described as starting at the top and going down, up and over, before tucking itself in.

These ideas may help solve some children's reversal problems before they become a major source of tension, when they are much harder to sort out. For many children mirror writing and b/d reversals are more an indication of inadequate teaching at the essential first stage of handwriting, than of anything wrong with the child. However, we must always be aware that more complex reversals or inverting of letters can be signalling deeper perceptual problems that do not disappear quickly, whatever exercises or explanations are given.

Some reversals, particularly at the end of words, may indicate directionality problems.

Writing posture

This section has dealt with letters in isolation to the body. All the instructions about helping children with their writing posture and paper position are specially relevant to children experiencing problems. Helping them to find an optimum writing position, perhaps with a slanting board, and allowing them a choice of pen or pencil will all make remedial help more effective. But the situation is usually more complicated than that; when children have automated an incorrect movement it is the body that has to relearn. Children may need to rehearse a new movement with much more of their body than just their fingers. From this perspective it can be seen how pencil hold and the resulting movement are interrelated. Children who push their letters upwards may have developed a 'pushing' way of holding a pencil to suit that 'away' movement. A two-pronged remedial attack may be needed, one through the letter movement that may allow the way the pencil is held to alter, and the other through the pencil hold and hand that may have to alter to help with the correct movement of the letters. None of this is easy. For everyone's sake it is so much better to get all of it right from the start.

37 Joining as soon as possible

Those who have never followed a policy similar to the one that has been suggested in this book may find what is said in this section hard to believe. Providing enough initial training has been done in the movement of letters, providing the children have been taught to have exit strokes on all the letters that terminate at the baseline, and providing thay have not been made to follow a strict model but permitted to adapt (within reason) to their own slant and letter proportion, almost all the children will find that the letters ending at the baseline begin to join spontaneously as the writers begin to relax and write faster. If the children are encouraged to join in this way and are praised when they do so, and not criticised if the result is not quite as neat as their separate letters, then many children can easily join the simple letters by the end of the first year of school.

Joins can be divided into family groups too. Those letters that join at the baseline; 'i,l,t,u,a,c,d,e,h,m,n', could be called spontaneous joins in that they can form automatically, but the other families have to be taught carefully. Teachers must decide which ones to teach first; the top joins from 'o,r,v,w', the crossbar join from 'f' (and sometimes 't'), and the reverse joins to the round letters, 'a,c,d,g,q'. One teacher reported that she always taught crossbar joins from the letters 'f' and 't' before any others, even baseline ones, because she felt that they were the easiest for children. Many teachers, perhaps under the influence of Marion Richardson feel that the reverse joins promote flow. They may find the 'cacaca' exercises easy themselves but not all young children have the same facility in producing this particular join, and it is children that we are considering here. With a 'join when comfortable attitude' it is often these reverse joins that are omitted and a penlift taken. This is because, apart from the awkward movement that is needed to go over the top of a round letter and back, that particular join is often not even very efficient.

Look what happened when this child's 'c' was formed, like her 'o', from the base upwards. Children must not be encouraged to join letters until the basic movement is correct.

The suggestion that is made here is that children should be taught all the families of joins in exercise form much as they were taught the original families of stroke related letters. It is not possible to give schools any firm directive about when these joins should be taught – but one indicator is perhaps relevant. At the pre-school stage if children are writing as much as their own name they should be taught the

Richard

Richard, age 7, had been restricted to neat separate letters.

Richard   Ric   Richa.

He wanted to join up the letters in his name, but got in a muddle.

ic   ch   ha   rd   Richard

Linking a pair at a time worked well, and he was soon joining happily.

correct movement of the letters in that name. If children are being encouraged to make spontaneous baseline joins they will soon start to experiment with joining their own name. As soon as that happens it is time to learn how to make those 'taught' joins properly.

The schools must decide their own policy for joins. Are they going to insist on every letter being joined, i.e. looped descenders, or are they going to promote a 'join when comfortable' attitude? Whichever option is decided should be discussed with the children so they understand what is expected of them, and how joins might help.

The families of joins

iltuhnmacdek	These letters join spontaneously at the baseline.
ft	'f' joins from the crossbar, 't' can also join this way.
orvw	These letters all join *from* the top.
acdgoq	The join *to* these letters goes over the top and back.
giyq	The first three letters can be left unjoined or loop from the descender. 'q's join is unique.
pb xz s	'p' and 'b' can join or not as you please. 'x' and 'z' are probably better not joined, and 's' joins more efficiently when simplified.

When joins are taught in this logical way children can easily see how they work. Already there are possibilities for discussion on such matters as whether to join certain letters ('r' is another one that is sometimes better left unjoined) and whether some letters need modifying before they can join efficiently.

Simple exercises for joins

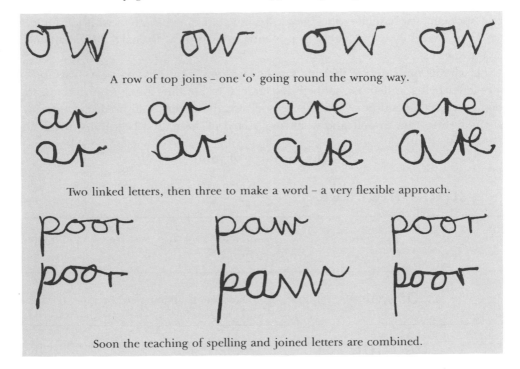

A page from a home-made copybook – joining from 'm'.

A row of top joins – one 'o' going round the wrong way.

Two linked letters, then three to make a word – a very flexible approach.

Soon the teaching of spelling and joined letters are combined.

Two more traditional copybooks (reduced), showing a horizontal and a vertical format.

Common digraphs and word endings make practical exercises.

Children need to be told that the joins probably help them to write faster, probably make it possible for them to develop a grown up handwriting, and probably make writing easier on their hands. It is not honest to be any more definite because many people manage throughout their lives with efficient and even mature looking separate letters. Children need to be told that their hands need a rest as they go along the page, so penlifts are desirable and nothing to be ashamed of even if the school has a 'continuous cursive' policy. It is always sad to see children whose hands need a penlift trying to disguise the fact by making a mock backward join. A lot of discussion is taking place at present about the desirability of having joined handwriting to help with spelling. This may be beneficial to spelling but at the stage that is under discussion words are likely to be limited to four or five letters. It is a serious matter to instill into young children the rule that every letter should be joined all the time regardless of comfort. When words elongate to twelve letters it can be a great strain on the hand. As with any other habit it is difficult to break.

One thing is certain: children should not be encouraged to join even a single pair of letters until all their letters move correctly. This requires constant vigilance on the part of teachers at this intermediate stage. Newcomers to the school may need to be held back from joining until any faults in letter movement can be retrained. There is no magic in joining for the sake of it, only in as much as joins may help people to write faster and more efficiently, and perhaps in a more mature manner.

This shows the destructiveness of using copybooks that require children to join every letter in long words. This girl is being criticised each time her writing signals that she would be better taking a pen-lift, or simplifying a letter such as 's'.

79

38 Personal letters lead to efficiency and speed

The aim of this section is to question traditional attitudes to certain aspects of teaching handwriting once the basic stages have been passed, and to ask why it is considered important for pupils to produce identical letterforms, in some cases up to quite a mature age, when we all accept the variability of adult handwriting. It is certainly not the intention to disrupt any method of teaching that succeeds for both teachers and pupils, merely to widen perspectives on handwriting and to ask everyone concerned to consider whether their strategies, even when they succeed at a particular stage in school life, meet all pupils' later needs.

The traditional approach to handwriting teaching was reassuring for teachers and probably for some pupils as well. The training was supposed to set the pupil on the right track by the copying of a carefully chosen model. The closer and the neater the pupil's reproduction of the model, the more praiseworthy. In the short term there was nothing wrong with that as long as teachers understood that as well as resembling the model in shape, the letters had first of all to commence in the right place and proceed in the correct direction – in other words, move correctly.

In the long term, however, various problems emerged; not the least being that once simplified models of separate letters became fashionable, it became extremely difficult to decide when a child should be allowed to alter to a more mature one. If the attitude was 'not until you are neat enough at printing', or 'not until everyone in the class is ready', then the real trouble began. Children today are encouraged to become creative, articulate and individual in their words. Once this change occurred in education, letters could no longer be expected to remain uniform – either within each child's work all the time, or between different writers. Young children struggling with spelling, grammar and the excitement of the ideas that they are trying to express, cannot be expected to keep up copybook letters at the same time.

These nine-year-olds show how soon pupils develop their own consistent slant and proportion if they are not taught too rigidly. Notice also their varied 'k's, particularly the bottom pair, where two different forms are used at the beginning and middle of the word

The written trace is a product of the hand, and is therefore influenced by how each individual uses their body. The more children have to struggle to copy a certain shape, slant or proportion which may not suit the way they use their hands, the less quickly they can automate the act of writing. Yet to achieve a way of writing that allows them to communicate their thoughts adequately, children need to be able to forget what their hands are doing and concentrate on the content of their work.

The purpose of a model, as seen by many people, is to ensure good quality, even beautiful handwriting, but is this really so? The very definition of 'good' handwriting varies from person to person, and many children, on the way to developing a good personal way of writing, do not follow the model. The more original and strong-minded the child, the more this would be likely to be reflected in their letters.

The variability of joins

Some people try to define exactly what is right and wrong about letters, but even this becomes almost impossible after the most basic of separate letters. Take a class where round, upright print script letters are taught and the emphasis is on neatness. Some children would be likely to find more efficient ways of quickly producing their letters than those that they were supposed to copy. Once the slant or proportion of letters is altered and, even minimally, the point of entry, the resulting joins would no longer be exactly the same as those from letters in the original model. They would however, probably be just as legible and more efficient for the writer concerned, which is what is important in the interests of a fast legible handwriting.

When joins are first taught to children there is still a strong case for their being taught in a formal way. In this book it has been explained how they can be taught in families, in this way building on to children's separate letters and accommodating slight differences in slant and proportion and even point of entry. Copybooks however, teach joined letters in a different way. By definition a copybook is meant to be copied so variations cannot be included. Copybooks are likely to use one particular form, for example of the letter 'f', and one recommended way of joining to and from it. If copybooks are marked, as they still are in many schools, then any letterform or join that is different to the copy must be wrong.

Ss⌐is says glass of
Peter and Paul are ten

There are many permissable stylistic variations. This writer displays two different forms of 'r' and several forms of 's'.

In countries that have strict national models where all children have to adhere to a model, perhaps right up until secondary school, it is often possible to see examples of a calligraphic standard of handwriting in pupils' exercise books. The letters remain standard and the joins as well, with no variations. This may be considered beautiful because of the regularity of the writing but problems arise later on because such children have never been allowed to develop any of the shortcuts that enable them to speed up their handwriting. The results of imposing discipline, rather than teaching self-discipline, can also be reflected in other behaviour at school.

81

Please do not think that I am recommending wildly variable, excessively untidy and increasingly illegible handwriting. To the contrary, considerable self-discipline is required to keep personal variations within the bounds of legibility. Teachers will need to be more knowledgeable, as well as more flexible about letterforms. A method that allows for experimentation is better than imposed discipline which stifles individuality and leaves the pupil without the strategies to develop a personal efficient hand. It also avoids the ugly confrontations that can occur, often with the most promising of pupils, when individuality is criticised.

There is a further problem in using a copybook technique for joined writing. Children should not and often cannot join every letter all the time; their hands need to rest and move along the line. How often they need a penlift may depend on the complexities of a particular sequence of letters as well as the size of letters.

In addition there are differences in the join itself which depend on the height and trajectory of the exit from the previous letter. Combine these 'built-in' differences with personal ones and the desirable aspects of the variations of letters become clearer. It is the benefits of such differences that concerns this section, and the awkward questions that they pose for teachers who intend to continue with a model orientated-policy, probably long after the advantage of such a system are outnumbered by the disadvantages.

Some letters lend themselves easily to efficient shortcuts, for instance 'f' and 'k'. Look at your own writing. Do your letterforms or your joins remain the same when the letter is at the beginning, the middle or the end of the word? The question that must be answered for children is should we encourage those who have found personal shortcuts and leave the others alone, or should we introduce all children to the idea that experimentation is a positive and desirable aspect of handwriting?

One more year in primary School
and we will be a First year
in Secondary School

The writer will need to relax and speed up this neat tight hand.

Double letters

Double letters could be a starting point for a lesson on the variability of joins. Start with simple ones, 'nn', 'll' and short words where there is unlikely to be much difference between the two letters. It might be worthwhile taking a count of how many pupils joined the pair, how many had straight terminals or curved exits on either letter. Longer words like 'mannequin' or 'appalled' might begin to show that even these pairs are not always written the same way. Penlifts sometimes occur when you stop to think about how to spell a word. Within 'cc', 'ee' or 'oo', the two letters may show subtle differences, caused by the height or trajectory of the previous exit.

nn ll cc ee tt ff oo ss

Double letters can lead to an understanding of personal joins.

coffee toffee coffee

Teaching double letters can help those still struggling to find an efficient form of a single 's', as well as 'ss' which often ends up in a magnificent tangle unless at least one letter is simplified. When it comes to 'tt' and 'ff' the fun begins. Try the pairs in words like 'coffee' and 'cliff', then let pupils exchange papers and attempt to copy each other's joins. This can be an interesting blackboard lesson, as there are a lot of different ways of joining when a crossbar is involved and it may be almost impossible to replicate another person's version.

The movement of the single 'f' is wrong, doubling it makes matters worse.

Those who have found individual shortcuts will delight in demonstrating them, and those who have not may be encouraged to try some for themselves. There will always be conventionally minded children, and if their choice is to keep close to the model, then that choice is valid for that child. At the other extreme there may be those who take too many shortcuts. They need to understand how this might erode the legibility of their handwriting.

Experimentation leads to an efficient joined 's' and a realisation that 'ss' often works better with a penlift.

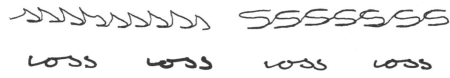

From an unhappy 'f' join to an efficient and graceful 'ff'.

Speed

Speeding-up exercises are intended to help writers to find efficient routes between letters. While children can do this consciously, designing themselves letters and joins that suit their hand, there is a deeper purpose to this exercise. Once a join has been performed by the movement of the hand when writing, that movement is stored in the motor memory. Once writing becomes automatic, using joins when comfortable if not all the time, the advantage of previous experimentation becomes evident. When extra speed is needed, the most efficient form of a letter in the required position is automatically retrieved from the motor memory to be brought into use. Try it yourself, write a phrase first slowly and neatly and then faster and faster until it becomes a tangled scribble. As likely as not many of the letters or joins will have simplified or even altered altogether during the speeding up. One of the most usual simplifications occurs in the letters 'th' in 'the'. This may help you to understand how helping children to speed up their letters can lead to more efficient handwriting. It may look a mess to start with, but with encouragement and informed assistance this can be the start of a handwriting that will serve that child when the demands for speed and quantity of written work increase.

I am looking for my cup of coffee on the

A slow print is this child's usual way of writing. Speeding up can help to promote efficiency.

I am looking for my cup of coffee on the table

Encouraged, she produced a few good joins, including a crossbar join in the word 'the'.

I am looking for my cup of coffee on the table

When asked to write the whole sentence faster and not to lift the pen between words she learned some more joins.

scissors   scissors   scissors

With one word 'scissors' treated in the same way, progress was made towards efficiency via a tangled 'ss'. There is plenty of room for improvement, but with help this girl should refine her letterforms and move ahead.

Do not be misled into thinking that there is any particular optimum speed. Children need to keep up with their thoughts, so fast thinkers can have trouble losing their train of thought as they struggle with their handwriting. It will not help if they are criticised for being less tidy than those who think more slowly and possibly more deeply, or those who are more economical with words. We accept that adults are different. We need to consider children and their handwriting in the same way.

39 What handwriting problems may indicate

If children have all been exposed to the same systematic teaching of handwriting and some have successfully picked it up whilst others have not, then both the diagnosis and remediation will need deeper thought. It is helpful to look at the situation in a slightly different way and to consider the handwriting as an indicator of problems. Then the written trace can be used as an aid to diagnosis, often revealing a child's underlying difficulty or condition.

Children do not all develop at the same speed and in the same way. Early handwriting problems may indicate nothing more than a slight delay in graphic or motor development. Many highly intelligent children may be articulate at an early age, musical or mathematically minded, but awkward and not as adept as their peers in the skills needed to acquire a flowing handwriting. Handwriting is no indication of intelligence, in fact the earliest developers often have most problems with the movement of letters. Such children often want to write before they have been taught properly, and in their haste to communicate their thoughts they have automated incorrect and often truncated letters that approximate to a visual representation of our alphabet. When you put handwriting into the right perspective, as a means of recording creative thought, it becomes clear that the younger the child, the wider the gap may be between their ideas, the skill and hand control needed to write them down.

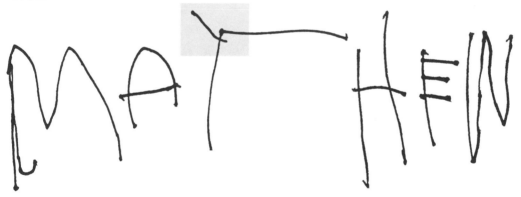

At five this child displayed his immature control through the construction of his capital letters, particularly the 'T' and 'E'. Two years later he was far ahead of all his classmates in mathematical and scientific subjects – but still had rather awkward handwriting.

Slow developers, in particular those with poor co-ordination, need to be brought on gently, and not criticised too much for their attempts before they are really ready to write. A systematic method helps them as long as they are allowed to repeat and reinforce each stage to develop their abilities at their own pace. Such children may surpass the early developers after a few years, when their real talents are recognised. In the meantime the main danger is an erosion of confidence from poor handwriting. Bad writing cannot be hidden. Self-criticism can be as destructive as that from outside. A word processor can be a great advantage for these children.

Poor spellers may often appear to write badly but frequently this is not the result of being unable to form their letters correctly. Constant hesitations and erasures disrupt the flow of writing; worry about spelling will cause tense writing, and some very poor spellers may end up reluctant to put anything down on paper. The converse may also be true – handwriting that does not flow may interrupt the sequencing of spelling. Keyboards will obviously benefit children who have spelling problems. It will help these children if they can see their ideas presented in a polished form occasionally. It is unlikely to be their fault that they are not able to learn to spell as easily as other children. Using a keyboard occasionally must not, and does not, mean that children should stop handwriting. It usually results in an improvement once the tension is lifted, by providing an alternative means of graphic communication.

thewasaladeinthehoowwithesuoma
and dog and sume pupes and s
a dog and wen seh sed srk and
sky came to her went and led on
her and seh sed to sry gow and
the blak bag and the leflit and
the bagg or a siker ro abig leflit

A word-processor was the temporary answer for this child who had considerable trouble with handwriting as well as with spelling.

There was a lady in the hall
with sume dogs and a dog kowd
Spark and the puppies came a
round the hall and the cildron
srk and   sky came to her went
and led on   her and seh sed to
sry gow and   the blak bag and
the leflit and the bagg or a siker

It allowed her to sort out her ideas in several drafts, without getting discouraged.

There was a lady in the hall
with some dogs and a dog
called Spark and the puppies
came around the hall and the
children stroked the puppies and
when we went out we got a
badge and got a bag or a sticker
or a leaflet or a big leaflet. We

This does not mean forgetting about handwriting. It encourages such children to record their ideas, while their other skills develop.

Handwriting can sometimes provide vital clues to certain medical conditions. Visual problems, for example, can remain undetected and affect the way a child writes. Regularly letter-spaced letters may indicate that a child cannot see to space them properly, but this is just as likely to indicate that the paper is in the wrong position so the writer cannot see what has just been written, as it is to indicate a need for an eye test. Uneven margins can also be an indication, though not always of anything serious. A change of paper position or angle may solve the problem, and only if the problem persists should further investigation be necessary.

A page like this, with widely spaced letters and a sloping margin should alert the teacher to the possibility that the child cannot see properly.

Uneven margins or writing on only one part of a page may signal visual or perceptual problems. Widely spaced letters may indicate that children cannot see what they have just written, in which case a change of paper position and slant may help.

Perceptual problems can affect how the child sees the world and can sometimes be spotted through handwriting. The solution may be quite commonsense, and just require a little extra patience and practice. Some perceptual difficulties, such as those of children who read better with the book upside down are difficult to detect in conventional eye tests. Such children have been adapting themselves since birth and may only become disorientated in specific tasks such as handwriting. These problems take time to correct themselves, and in the meantime children need understanding and sympathy while they wrestle with a problem that is little understood.

Where tension is indicated either by the child's handwriting, excessive pressure on the paper, or by any part of the body it should be taken into account. Tension, sometimes severe enough to result in a tremor, may be indicating too much pressure

At school entry.

After one term.

At six years old.

At seven years old.

A tremor at five might indicate something serious. With this child it must have only been caused by tension because his handwriting developed well and two years later it was flowing and mature.

on young children. Less pressure and plenty of praise while they relax and catch up in whatever field of learning is proving difficult, may be more useful than extra handwriting teaching. On the other hand tense hands and bodies may be reflecting problems such as a marriage breaking up at home or a bereavement. The school cannot cure such matters but they need to be taken into account, and allowance made at such times. Unfortunately the effect of tension on handwriting can produce the uneven, jagged, and often downright ugly letters that invite criticism or suggest the need for exercises to correct what is at that moment beyond the power of the child to remedy.

An alert class teacher may spot difficulties that left undiagnosed can cause a child untold misery. A more detailed account of handwriting as an indicator of problems appears in this book's companion volume, *Handwriting: a new perspective* (Stanley Thornes (Publishers) Ltd, 1990).

Michael 9 This is my best writing.

My names is Karen I am ten years old.

Small tense handwriting often invites criticism. As this tension is an indication of the child's condition, such criticism is only likely to make matters worse.

40 Conclusion

Now it is up to teachers to put these ideas into practice in their own way. I cannot guarantee that all or any of these suggestions will work in isolation. Nothing can be proven in such a complicated situation, just as in the past it has never been possible to prove that any particular model has worked successfully. All I can say is that for the past decade my weeks have been taken up by looking at handwriting problems all over the world. My weekends, wherever I have been, have been full of children and adults with handwriting problems all seeking advice. Many of them were suffering pain and unable to write for want of some commonsense remarks about writing posture; or else they needed to relax both physically and about the standard that they expected of their handwriting at speed. Some children have been 'cured' by allowing them to choose their own pen, have some fun and overcome their fear of writing. Some needed to be told to join their letters more, others not to join them so much. Some have had to be told to pay no attention to their school or even their parents who may have insisted on change or improvement in what was already a perfectly serviceable tool for communication. The message throughout all this parade of suffering was clear: none of the systems of teaching handwriting were meeting present day needs; something had to be done.

I never intended to get involved in handwriting, but was lured away from an interesting design practice by the desperate situation in a field in which, having been trained as a professional scribe, I had some of the necessary skills. More important still I had watched my own children and their contemporaries struggle against model- and neatness-orientated teaching methods that worked against their best interests as creative individuals.

Now it is for other people to take up the challenge. Let them use what is relevant from this book and its companion volume, *Handwriting: a new perspective,* to evolve policies that work for their districts, schools and above all children, in varying situations. There is going to be a need for flexible attitudes and open but informed minds to deal with the rapidly altering situation in education and technology over the next few years.

Handwriting posture can also provide clues to a child's disabilities, visual ones in particular.

Index